THE DEFINITIVE GUIDE
to *the*
OPPOSITE SEX
A Men's Guide to Women

by Nicholas Pashley and Anthony Jenkins

Eden Press

The Definitive Guide to the Opposite Sex

ISBN: 1-55045-010-7

© Pacquet De L'Editeur Eden

Cover cartoon: Tony Jenkins

Cover design: Pamela Chichinskas & Lynette Stokes

Printed in Canada at Metropole Litho
Depot légal — premier trimestre 1989
Bibliothèque nationale du Quebec

Eden Press
31A Westminster Avenue
Montreal, Quebec H4X 1Y8

Canadian Cataloguing in Publication Data

Main entry under title:
    The Definitive guide to the opposite sex

Is comprised of two publications, back to back:
    A Woman's guide to men / by Pamela
    Chichinskas and Lynette Stokes; A Man's guide
    to women / by Tony Jenkins and Nicholas Pashley.
ISBN 1-55045-010-7

1. Sex role--Humor.   2. Men--Humor.   3. Women--
Humor.   4. Interpersonal relationships--Humor.
I. Chichinskas, Pamela   II. Stokes, Lynette
III. Jenkins, Anthony   IV. Pashley, Nicholas
IV. Title: A Woman's guide to men. V. Title:
A Man's guide to women.

PN6231.S54D44 1989   818'.5402'08   C89-090090-6

TABLE OF CONTENTS

FOREWORD
by Anthony Jenkins 7

A FEW PERCEPTIVE THINGS THAT HAVE BEEN SAID ABOUT WOMEN
by Nicholas Pashley 8

INTRODUCTION
by Nicholas Pashley and Anthony Jenkins................................9

MEN AND WOMEN: HOW TO SPOT THE DIFFERENCE
by Nicholas Pashley 11

LADIES' LIMERICKS
by Anthony Jenkins 14

WHAT DO WOMEN WANT?
by Nicholas Pashley 15

AURAL SEX
by Anthony Jenkins 18

WOMEN AND SEX: A BEGINNER'S GUIDE FOR BOYS
by Nicholas Pashley 21

WOMEN'S ARTS PRIMER
by Anthony Jenkins 23

MALE VICTIMS OF FEMALE VIOLENCE
by Nicholas Pashley 25

GUIDE TO WOMEN'S BODIES
by Anthony Jenkins 28

WOMEN'S TEN COMMANDMENTS
by Anthony Jenkins 30

WOMEN AND SEX: AN INTERMEDIATE GUIDE FOR BOYS
by Nicholas Pashley 31

WOMEN'S LIFE PATHS
by Anthony Jenkins 34

WHAT FACE SHAPE DO YOU HAVE?
by Anthony Jenkins 36

WOMEN AND FAT
by Nicholas Pashley 37

WOMEN AND LOVE
by Nicholas Pashley 39

GREAT MOMENTS IN THE HISTORY (AND FUTURE) OF WOMANHOOD
by Anthony Jenkins 41

WHAT WOMEN TALK ABOUT
by Nicholas Pashley 45

BIKINI WAXING EXPLAINED
by Anthony Jenkins 48

3 REASONS TO BE GLAD THAT MEN DON'T SUFFER FROM PMS
by Anthony Jenkins 50

WOMEN AND MARRIAGE
by Nicholas Pashley 51

WHY DO WOMEN BOTHER?
by Anthony Jenkins 54

TALKING TO WOMEN
by Nicholas Pashley 57

MS. GOOSE: NON-SEXIST NURSERY RHYMES
by Anthony Jenkins 59

LADIES' NOBEL PRIZES
by Anthony Jenkins 62

WHAT DO WOMEN KNOW?
by Nicholas Pashley 63

WOMEN'S UNDER-SHIRT BRA-REMOVAL SECRET REVEALED
by Anthony Jenkins 65

WOMEN'S CONTRIBUTION TO SCIENCE
by Anthony Jenkins 68

THE SEX OBJECT CONTROVERSY
by Nicholas Pashley 69

10 CAN'T-MISS LINES TO USE ON WOMEN
by Nicholas Pashley 71

MR. RIGHT
by Anthony Jenkins 72

FOREWORD

Julio Perez de Gonad

First Secretary
United Nations Council for the Advancement
of Women's Rights

Hey Mamma!

    Loooking gooood! My, my my! Tasty! Yeah!
Oooh yeah! Like the way you walk, foxy mamma!
Yeahh! Shake it, but don't break it! Va-va-
voom! Come to pappa!

    Hope you like this book. You gonna love
it. I know what you like.

    But you wanna have some real laughs, you
come see Julio. Anytime! Yeah! I got what
you need!

                              Oooh yeah!
                              Anytime!

A FEW PERCEPTIVE THINGS THAT HAVE BEEN SAID ABOUT WOMEN

"A woman is necessarily an evil, but he that gets the most tolerable one is lucky." — Menander

"A woman is the last thing that will be civilized by man." — George Meredith

"Such duty as the subject owes the prince,
Even such a woman oweth to her husband."
— William Shakespeare

"What mighty ills have not been done by women!
Who was't betrayed the Capital? — A woman!
Who lost Marc Antony the world? — A woman!
Who was the cause of a long ten years' war,
And laid at last old Troy in ashes? — Woman!
Destructive, damnable, deceitful woman! " — Thomas Otway

"Women do not find it difficult nowadays to behave like men; but they often find it extremely difficult to behave like gentlemen." — Compton Mackenzie

"That's the thing about girls. Every time they do something pretty, even if they're not much to look at, or even if they're sort of stupid, you fall half in love with them, and then you never know *where* the hell you are." — J. D. Salinger

"According to recent studies, those men who don't understand women fall into two groups: bachelors and husbands." — Jacques Languirand

INTRODUCTION

Women — don't you love 'em? We've called them a lot of things over the years: girls, chicks, dames, broads, skirts, babes, fillies, dolls, just to name a few. Nowadays, of course, we have to call them women, but we don't mind. Pop stars call them "lady" quite frequently, but in real life "lady" seems slightly ridiculous for anyone not wearing white gloves. So we call them women now. Which is fine with us. They can be called any damn thing they like, just because they're so goshdarned cute.

Well aren't they? Look at their cute little noses, and their cute little feet, and the cute things they do with their hair. Listen to their cute high voices and the cute things they say, like: "Oooooh yucko!" or "That Tom Cruise is just the most scrumptious thing I ever saw!!!" Even when they go out into the real world and get real, serious jobs in banks and law firms, they still wear those cute little bows around their necks, and they won't leave home until they've got them just so.

Face it, they can't help being cute. They've got the cutest smiles you can imagine. And when they get mad?! Hold me back!! Their little cheeks go all red, and their little teeth get all clenched up, and their little brows furrow like one of those silly dogs with no hair, and they say cute things like, "Oh, for God's sake Roger, you're so infantile!" or "I'm practically a vice-president; don't call me a girl!" or "Is that all you ever think about?"

Women have cute names. Stephanie. Debbie. Peggy-Sue. Nadine. Midge. Cute as buttons, every one of them. Even the tough-talking, death-to-male-things feminists have cute names. Gloria. Betty. Germaine. Andrea. You see what I mean? They just can't help it.

Not that we want them to. No sir, we like them just the way they are. Cute little shoulders, cute little calves, cute little belly buttons, you name it. They've got those cute little running shoes with the little tiny socks with the pom-poms at the heel. And don't get me started on knee socks! And isn't it cute the way the world's going seriously to hell, what with the ozone layer, mass starvation, and the Middle East, and women are still going about worrying about love and matching plates. Now that's cute!

9

And that's why we love them. That's why men are prepared to endure the moods, the nonsense, the recriminations, and the incessant talk about dieting. We can't help it; we're slaves to cuteness. Oh, and by the way, you don't have to call us men, if you don't want to. You can call us guys or dudes or studs or fellows or blokes or chaps or hunks. We don't mind. Just don't call us late for dinner, you hear?

Nicholas Pashley

Welcome to the MEN'S HALF of this book. Traditionally, and somewhat jokingly, a wife is referred to as a man's "better half." Not so in literature. The "better half" of any cooperative published work is the part written by men. This book is yet another example of that. As the better half, this is also the FRONT of *The Definitive Guide to the Opposite Sex.* Behind any great man is a good woman, and in back of every great humor book is some twaddle written by women. But let us not be ungenerous to our coauthoresses: they try hard, serve a lovely souffle, and are dynamite in bed.

Testosteronely yours,
Anthony Jenkins

MEN AND WOMEN HOW TO SPOT THE DIFFERENCE

If we are to proceed any further with this discussion of women, we should attempt to make it clear that we can distinguish between women and men. As recently as the Sixties, we learned that the length of hair was no longer a reliable landmark of sexual determination. Before that, the wearing of trousers had long ceased to be an exclusively masculine trait. Nowadays, of course, the carrying of leather bags and the wearing of fur coats by men has become commonplace.

So, how can we tell women from men any more? It is not as difficult as it might appear. For starters, there are character traits that remain fairly constant. Men, for instance, are honorable, straight-dealing, companionable, and even-tempered. Women, on the other hand, are flighty, perfidious, moody, and calculating. None of this is intended to place any judgment on men and women; this is simple scientific observation.

Women, it should also be noted, are alluring and mysterious. To achieve these qualities, of course, they spend most of their disposable income on little jars and bottles of stuff that men — naive fools that we are — know little about. This is why men have to pay for dinner; women cannot afford to be alluring and mysterious and still feed themselves.

There are many mysterious things about women. Women are prey to arcane physical ailments that men are not permitted to inquire about. Despite these frequent ailments, as well as an innate flimsiness that precludes activities like standing up, walking, or carrying things, women outlive men in this society by more than seven years. This may be in some part due to their being better rested than men.

To return to the subject, however. The couple in Figure 1. demonstrate some of the obvious differences between men and women. Her hair has been the object of much care, and her clothing reflects a feminine delight in frippery. Her distinctive costume is impractical to the point that she must hang on to part of it while dancing.

11

He, on the other hand, is imprisoned inside conventional male garb that has been forced upon him by a female-dominated society. Who is it that broods about what people wear? Women. Who is it that says, as a couple is preparing for an evening out, "You're not going out in *that*?!" Women! Our gentleman friend in the illustration is attempting to dance while corseted in a tight collar and heavily starched shirtfront. His ruffled, thinning hair gives some idea of the difficulty.

Look at their faces. He is stressed, anxious, probably still concerned about some real crisis in the workplace as he attempts to accommodate

Figure 1.

the needs of his pleasure-seeking female companion. She, meanwhile, bears a look of calm serenity. She has this man where she wants him. If she tires of him, she can quickly find another. Perhaps even a taller one. With a bosom of those proportions, she is clearly in the driver's seat.

Now, let us proceed with caution. Many people find it easier to distinguish between women and men when the people in question are undressed. There are indeed a handful of basic anatomical differences between the sexes that generally make identification almost foolproof. We have, at no small expense, succeeded in persuading a man and a woman of our acquaintance to remove their clothing and demonstrate these differences. The illustrations thus procured are not intended to titillate or offend. They are intended for adult viewing only, and merely as an educational tool. If you have a letter of consent from a parent or guardian, we may continue.

Figure 2. displays basic male anatomy. Note the distinctive moustache and the well-developed muscularity, both classic masculine

features. This
gentleman's charisma
and appeal have been
heightened by use of
the Duchaine Univer-
sal Negative Ion
Generating Belt
(available for a short
time only at $29.95,
payable to Eden Press;
act now — operators
are standing by to take
your call). The viewer can see the
robust heartiness, the fundamental
decency of manliness in this illustration, although the absence of
underarm hair does smack of
subterfuge.

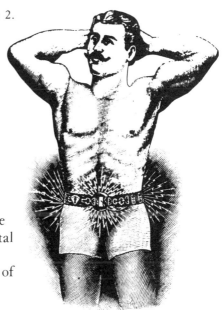

Figure 2.

In Figure 3. we see revealed
the glories of the feminine form.
Gosh. A bit of all right, eh? Further comment would seem
superfluous, although we should
point out that the woman in question has an M.B.A. from a very
good school and is on the fast track
at a major brokerage firm. A vice-
presidency is not out of the question. She has written a best-selling
novel, has had a one-woman show
of her sculpture at a leading New
York gallery, and represented her
country at the 1988 Seoul Olym-
pics. A Sagittarius, Tracey enjoys
skiing and surfboarding, and is
crazy for guys who look like Jon
Bon Jovi.

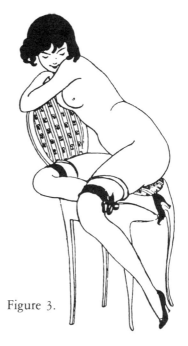

Figure 3.

Now then, if you feel you have a handle on the ways in which
women are different from men — and you're not too agitated over
these provocative illustrations — you are ready to continue.

LADIES' LIMERICKS

Men, women aren't the delicate damsels and shrinking violets they once were. No frigging way! They're rough, tough and in the buff; smoking cigars, getting tattooed, and indulging in locker room banter that would shock the pants off a drunken stevedore. The phrase "not in mixed company" means diddly squat today and to the shame of us all, the fair sex has staked out a claim in the last motherlode of male-dominated crudity, the limmerick, unless men can popularize something even cruder, like French kissing your grandmother, for example. Read 'em and weep.

There was a young boy doll named Ken,
Who for Barbie had a great yen.
He proceeded to maul her,
And said he would call her,
And didn't. Just typical! Men!

There once was a Mister named Right,
Whose girl he would nibble and bite,
He was a real prince,
And ignored the flab dints,
Fat hips and thick cellulite.
(And he was a lawyer)

There once was a feminists' convention
That was rife with strife and dissention
The sisters were wise,
Not chauvinist guys,
But all suffered from premenstrual tension.

If only men weren't such fools,
Who thought with their brains, not their tools,
If only a cock
Had a biological clock
And we both played with the same set of rules.

There once was a lady named Cash,
Who thought marrying men was quite rash,
But she, with regret,
Could not forget
That dildoes can't take out the trash.

WHAT DO WOMEN WANT?

Well, there's the zillion-dollar question. Freud wondered about that one too, and he wasn't the first, not by a long shot. Adam, we can be sure, did not go unperplexed by Eve. What did Eve want? The one thing in the whole damn garden she wasn't supposed to have, and the rest is history. Some damn serpent comes along and sweet-talks Eve into falling off her diet, and the rest of us have been paying the price ever since. Charming!

So what do women want, now that they can have all the apples they want? Well, to listen to them talk, the last thing they want is men. We all overhear conversations from time to time, and it's no secret that women do a lot of complaining about men. We're insincere, we never call, we drink too much, we don't notice when they get their hair done, we look at other women, we'd rather watch baseball games than clean the basement, we don't talk about our feelings, and we stink up the bathroom. Fair enough. That's what men are like. If you don't like them, don't get one.

But they still want one. Their mothers have warned them about us, but even their mothers want them to have one. In fact, their mothers would rather they had a bad one than no man at all. OK, historically it made sense. Men made all the money and were good at fixing things. A husband was a useful thing for a woman. He could buy her things, and if they broke, he could repair them. And bathrooms always smelled in those days anyway.

Modern man is not very good at fixing things. Modern things aren't meant to be fixed. You throw them out and buy new ones, but you need two incomes to afford them. So the woman has to go out and work, thus defeating the purpose of having men in the first place.

So, back to square one. What do they want us for? All right, bub, I see you smirking. I know what you're thinking. The big S-E-X, right? You think she goes all weak in the knees at the sight of you in your jockey shorts. Ha! Don't kid yourself, mister. We'll get to that later. Just take a look at women's magazines and what do you see? Big macho hunks with bulging blue jeans? Not even close. Women's magazines — just like men's magazines — are full of photographs of attractive women, so figure that out.

15

Which is not to say that women don't think about sex. They are almost human, after all. They just don't think about it at the same time you do. And when they think about it . . . well, just go back to their conversations about men. What do women want? They want sensitive guys with good minds, a gentle sense of humor, and a lot of warmth and understanding, right? Wrong again. They want some football player with eyes about a millimeter apart, a hairline that starts right above the said eyes, and a twenty-two-inch neck. Fortunately, most of these guys kill themselves in Camaros before the age of twenty, so the majority of women are in fact stuck with guys like us.

And, of course, they're damn lucky to get us. There are more of them than there are of us, after all. The great love of young men for contact sports, fast cars, and weapons leaves the male segment of the species a trifle depleted by the age of twenty. In addition, our tremendous workload and competitive lifestyle — while we toil to purchase the microwave ovens and lettuce dryers that make the modern woman's life worthwhile — leave us frequently dead at fifty. All of which means that the relative handful of men who remain are at something of a premium (and half of those appear to have gone off women in any case).

So there's the economic law of supply and demand, which may account for some of the attraction we hold for womenfolk. But there must be more than that. After all, if it were simply scarcity that motivated women, they'd all be trying to buy Maseratis, which is not the case.

So what is it? Why do women want to have a man? Extensive research has finally revealed the true story. It is no longer — in an era when any intelligent woman can earn at least as much as the average man — a need for financial security. Nor has it anything to do with a fascination for the male sexual organ — an anatomical oddity our correspondents have described in terms that ranged from "ludicrous and inadequate" to "creepy and grotesque."

We return to the original question. What do women want? Answer — a man. Why? Because other women will make fun of them if they don't have one. This is absolutely true. Just about every woman in this culture went to high school. To this day — however long it's been — she is aware that at any time she might run into an old high school girlfriend, and the first question is going to be, "So, are you married?"

There is no question of this. Every woman in the western world, with the possible exception of Janis Joplin, experienced a moment of panic at some point in high school when she realized that, whatever else she did in life, she would be regarded as a failure by other women if she didn't bag a husband. And that is why, to this day, intelligent women with goals and careers will throw themselves at the most unsuitable men imaginable. Which, if you're a man, increases your chances of getting a date on Saturday night.

(See also **Women and Marriage,** and **What Women Talk About.**)

Women almost never listen, but they sure like to talk, talk, talk.
They are by far the more

AURAL SEX

THINGS WOMEN WILL NEVER SAY

THINGS WOMEN LIKE TO HEAR

DON'T LIKE TO HEAR

WOMEN AND SEX
A Beginner's Guide for Boys

By now you will have absorbed a little about what women want, how they are different from you, and you have been told what women like to hear. Now you are ready for what men have traditionally called Having Sex, women have called Falling in Love, and what is now widely known as Establishing a Relationship.

Now, boys, you may have noticed — at least the more observant among you — that girls of your age have in the last year or so developed a sort of curvaceousness to their bodies. This is perfectly natural, and should not be the cause of lewd speculation on your part. You may also have noticed a slight change in your attitude towards these girls. Whereas a year ago you may have thought of them as "yucky" or simply not very good at sports, you may have begun to see them in a new light. This is also perfectly natural, and should not be a cause for concern.

Perhaps you have experienced a tightening of the throat when speaking to girls, or perhaps a weakening in the knees. This was once known as "coming over all queer," which now means something altogether different, and nothing at all to do with girls. You may also have noticed a certain physiological change in one of the more brutish parts of your body. This effect is likely to occur in more extreme circumstances: being either awake or asleep, for instance, or being alive on a day of the week ending in a "y." While this syndrome is perfectly natural, it is not to be encouraged. It can usually be quelled by concentrating hard on no-nonsense subjects like algebra or physics.

These physical phenomena, which may be happening to you when you talk to a girl, or even when you think of one, are your body's way of telling you that you want to "have sex" with this girl, or, very likely, any girl at all. Well, this is all very well for you, but not so nice for the girl. Girls are concerned with finer things, with beauty — flowers, pretty paintings, baby animals, and the like. The last thing they want to think about is you and your nasty little thing.

Perhaps years from now, when you are married, your wife will permit you to "have sex" with her, in gratitude for some good deed on your part — cleaning out the eavestroughing, for example, or refinishing an old but valued item of furniture. In this event, it is considered good manners to "finish off" as quickly as possible and apologize afterwards. The secret to a successful marriage is mutual respect, and it is unlikely that your wife will respect you if you are forever pointing your beastly, unattractive "little chap" at her.

Remember, boys — girls are delicate creatures, and they have more important things to worry about than being "bothered" by little savages like yourselves. Now, if there are no questions, let us return to geometry.

WOMEN'S ARTS PRIMER

GRAPHIC ART: Women like to draw horses; they are man substitutes — something strong and wild to wrap your legs around — without the emotional baggage. Practice sketching horses like those below. To show you are especially sensitive, draw them galloping in open fields of wildflowers. Studiously avoid any representation of genitalia.

POETRY: Compose an eight-line, two stanza poem about your "innermost feelings." Write it in fountain pen and smudge it slightly with a tear or two.

Mention the following:

Soaring birds (especially doves)
Horses running free
Hearts overflowing or bursting
The words 'silken' or 'flaxen,'
or 'gilded'
Falling leaves
Spring or autumn
Sunsets, crashing waves, dewdrops
like tears

Avoid the following:

Toxic waste
Basketball
Jehovah's Witnesses
Piston rings

SHORT STORIES: Practice writing painfully romantic short stories on pastel note paper. Feature sensitive women in anguish finally meeting Mr. Right, who has been waiting for a girl like them all his life. Make sure to finish with everyone's hearts "overflowing with love they have never known before." Submit the results to the "This Month's Short Story" editor of major women's magazines.

Include in the plot:
* Cute spellings of all women's names (Caryle, Krystle, etc.)
* Long form of all men's names (Edward, Richard — never Ed, Dick). No Bernies, Roscos
* A sensitive heroine who weeps every night at home alone
* A tough, yet tender man, who hides his emotions in skydiving, auto racing, bullfighting, and similar masculine pursuits
* A kindly father in a sweater
* Lonely, motherless little boy from the father's first, tragic relationship
* Full, sensuous lips
* A single tear on a pillow
* A first kiss (must be smoldering or lingering)
* An exhilarating ride in a fast sports car/galloping steed/horse-drawn sleigh
* A heart "beating so hard she can scarcely speak"
* Rain, falling leaves, and stormy nights

MALE VICTIMS OF FEMALE VIOLENCE

Sugar and spice and all things nice
That's what little girls are made of

You can't stay married in a situation where you are afraid to
go to sleep in case your wife might cut your throat.
Mike Tyson

We are accustomed to thinking of women as the gentler sex. This is merely one of our bigger mistakes. (Fortunately it can usually be cured through intensive exposure to footage of Margaret Thatcher's speeches.) Still, the notion persists that women are fundamentally harmless, probably because of their attachment to young fur-bearing animals and ballet. We must not be deceived. In 1983, there were a record 19,019 women housed in U.S. state or federal prisons. Even in peace-loving Canada, 1985 saw 7,033 adult females charged with violent crime, including 153 charges of homicide or attempted murder. Murderous women are everywhere. And it is a known fact that most of them get acquitted on the Premenstrual Syndrome defense. "I'm sorry, judge, I was feeling a little cranky that day." The following is merely a partial list of men who have been the victims of violent women.

* The sons of Greek hero Jason, slain by their flighty mother Medea. Medea, as it turns out, was not the nicest person to be related to, having previously killed her brother Absyrtus and chopped him up into little pieces.

* Greek warrior Agamemnon, stabbed by his wife Clytemnestra in roughly 1180 B.C., according to Aeschylus. Clytemnestra and her fancy man, Aegisthus, were later killed by daughter Electra and her brother Orestes. This sort of family bloodletting was not unknown among the Greeks. The Romans were no better. Empress Livia Drusilla accounted for numerous members of her family before dying peacefully in her bed in her mid-eighties.

* Sisera, captain of the Canaanite army, slain by Jael, wife of Heber the Kenite, with a tent peg through the temple in about 1100 B.C. (Judges 4). Interestingly, most of the women who are actually named in the Bible are not what Beaver Cleaver's mother would have called Nice Girls. Nice Girls, like all

the women in the story of Noah, for instance, are generally anonymous. The women with names are usually harlots, but there is the occasional man-killer, like the clever Jael with her lethal tent peg. II Chronicles 22 tells of Athaliah, a particularly cranky piece of work, who slew as many of the male heirs of the house of Judah as she could find, before getting her comeuppance in II Chronicles 23. Judith, of the apocryphal Old Testament book of that name, was a Nice Girl who consented to visit the warrior Holofernes in his tent, then hacked his head off.

* John the Baptist, beheaded at the request of Salomé, *circa* 30 A.D. The first recorded case of a man losing his head to an exotic dancer.

*John Rogers, Protestant martyr, the first of some 300 burned at the stake between 1555 and 1558 by "Bloody" Mary, Queen of England. This 45-month slaughter is the longest continuous incidence of Premenstrual Syndrome on record. Yet even Bloody Mary was outdone by the highly cultured Catherine de Medici who instigated the Massacre of St. Bartholomew, a lively event that saw some 50,000 French Huguenots slaughtered in 1572. Mary and Catherine give some suggestion of the danger of dating Catholic girls.

* Henry Darnley, blown up and strangled at the instigation of his wife, Mary Queen of Scots, on February 9, 1567. Mary's lifelong rival, Elizabeth I, had her ex-boyfriend, Robert Devereux, Earl of Essex, executed on February 25, 1601.

*French revolutionary and scientist Jean Paul Marat, stabbed in his bath, July 13, 1793, by Charlotte Corday (played in the film by Glenda Jackson).

* Johnny, shot and fatally wounded by Frankie, according to the popular song, *circa* 1870. He was her man, but he allegedly done her wrong. See also Cole Porter's Miss Otis, a society dame who regretfully had to miss lunch as a result of being up on a murder rap.

* Andrew Jackson Borden, recipient of forty whacks with an axe wielded by his daughter Lizzie, August 4, 1892. Having seen what she had done, the perpetrator allegedly gave her mother (actually stepmother) forty-one.

* American mobster Johnny Stompanato, stabbed to death by Cheryl Crane, teenaged daughter of Lana Turner, April 4, 1958.

* Singer Sam Cooke, shot and killed by Bertha Franklin, December 10, 1964.

* Andy Warhol, shot and critically wounded by Valerie Solanas, founder of SCUM — Society for Cutting Up Men, June 3, 1968.

* President Gerald R. Ford, victim of unsuccessful assassination attempt by Lynette (Squeaky) Fromme, September 5, 1975. Seventeen days later, Ford was again the target of a futile effort, this time by Sara Jane Moore.

* Diet expert Dr. Herman Tarnower, fatally shot by socialite Headmistress Jean Harris, March 10, 1980.

* John Belushi, given fatal drug overdose by Canadian *femme fatale* Cathy Evelyn Smith, March 5, 1982.

* In addition, thousands of British Members of Parliament, captains of industry, and senior civil servants have been the victims of brutal spankings performed by usually anonymous women wearing schoolgirl uniforms. (It is believed that few, if any, of these women are in fact schoolgirls.)

GUIDE TO WOMEN'S BODIES

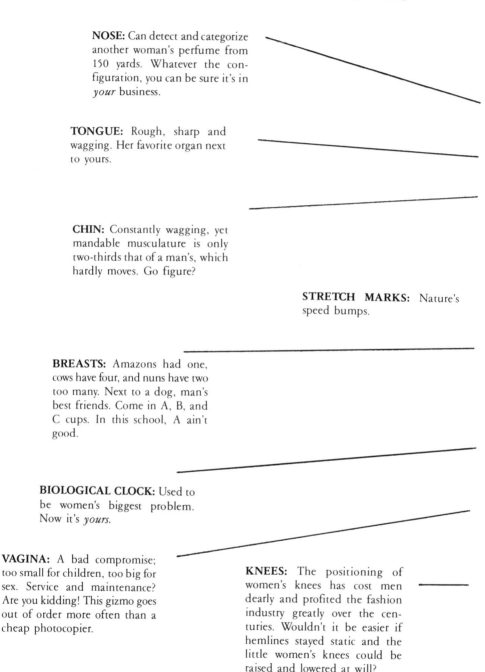

NOSE: Can detect and categorize another woman's perfume from 150 yards. Whatever the configuration, you can be sure it's in *your* business.

TONGUE: Rough, sharp and wagging. Her favorite organ next to yours.

CHIN: Constantly wagging, yet mandable musculature is only two-thirds that of a man's, which hardly moves. Go figure?

STRETCH MARKS: Nature's speed bumps.

BREASTS: Amazons had one, cows have four, and nuns have two too many. Next to a dog, man's best friends. Come in A, B, and C cups. In this school, A ain't good.

BIOLOGICAL CLOCK: Used to be women's biggest problem. Now it's *yours.*

VAGINA: A bad compromise; too small for children, too big for sex. Service and maintenance? Are you kidding! This gizmo goes out of order more often than a cheap photocopier.

KNEES: The positioning of women's knees has cost men dearly and profited the fashion industry greatly over the centuries. Wouldn't it be easier if hemlines stayed static and the little women's knees could be raised and lowered at will?

WOMEN'S INTUITION: A brain substitute. A sort of feminine cerebral NutraSweet.

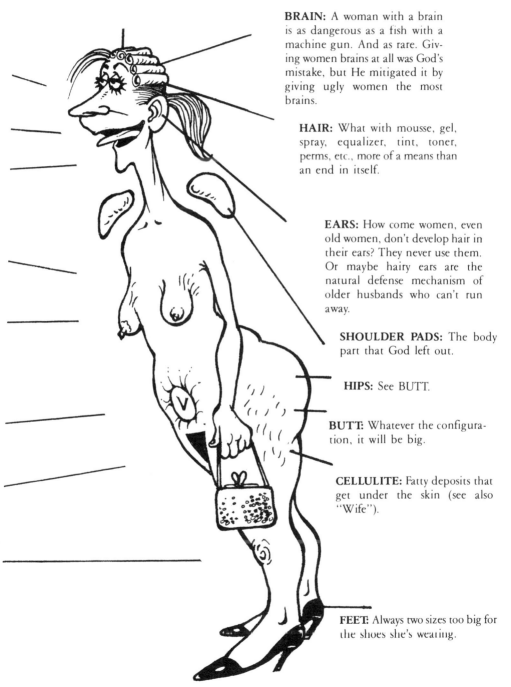

BRAIN: A woman with a brain is as dangerous as a fish with a machine gun. And as rare. Giving women brains at all was God's mistake, but He mitigated it by giving ugly women the most brains.

HAIR: What with mousse, gel, spray, equalizer, tint, toner, perms, etc., more of a means than an end in itself.

EARS: How come women, even old women, don't develop hair in their ears? They never use them. Or maybe hairy ears are the natural defense mechanism of older husbands who can't run away.

SHOULDER PADS: The body part that God left out.

HIPS: See BUTT.

BUTT: Whatever the configuration, it will be big.

CELLULITE: Fatty deposits that get under the skin (see also "Wife").

FEET: Always two sizes too big for the shoes she's wearing.

WOMEN'S TEN COMMANDMENTS

1. I am the Acquisitive Bitch-Goddess. Thou shalt have no gods before me.

2. Remember Boxing Day, and keep it open.

3. Thou shalt not take the name of anyone present in vain.

4. Honor thy hairstylist and thy gynecologist.

5. (In the presence of thy boyfriend's ex-girlfriend) thou shalt dress to kill.

6. Thou shalt never tip more than five percent.

7. Thou shalt haggle over the bill.

8. Thou shalt keep him waiting.

9. Thou shalt not covet thy neighbor's husband (unless she's a real bitch and deserves it).

10. Thou shalt not covet thy neighbor's credit limit.

WOMEN AND SEX
An Intermediate Guide for Boys

Well, boys, it's been a year or so since I last spoke to you on the subject of what President Bush would most likely call "the sex thing." Some of you have come to me with questions, and I would be remiss if I were to leave these questions unanswered.

First of all, I have been asked if masturbation is wrong. Yes, it is. Will it make you go blind? Yes, it will. I trust that will be an end to that.

Now, some of the more precocious of you have been told that it is possible to "have sex" — as we say — with a woman without actually marrying her. While such an act is, of course, morally repugnant, it is technically possible. I do not condone it, but I have been asked to explain how it might occur, how you should conduct yourself, and how much it will cost.

I should begin by pointing out that in "having sex" with someone to whom you are not married you are running the risk of coming into contact with a Bad Woman. This may have untold repercussions if you should choose a career in public service or the church. Girls, I should tell you, are impetuous creatures who love to talk, particularly to reporters, and if your name should accidentally slip out in conversation you could find yourself in an embarrassing spot.

Now, as to "having sex." Yes, in answer to one question, it is possible to pay for it. This involves locating someone who is willing to perform certain acts in return for cash. These persons are known as "ladies of the night," "prostitutes," or "hookers." While they are not necessarily Bad Women, they are seldom what your mother might call "Nice Girls." "Nice Girls" have sex — as we say — only when they are what they call "in love."

Dealing with professional women — and I am not speaking here of female lawyers or doctors — carries with it certain risks of both a legal and medical nature, which we will not get into here. Suffice it to say, however, that if you regard your body as a temple — which by the looks of most of you seems unlikely — you will avoid such persons, quite literally like the plague.

What is it, Jackson? You wonder if it is always easy to tell whether a woman is a prostitute? Generally speaking, a prostitute does not require dinner beforehand. A woman who continues to chew gum through the sexual act is usually, though not always, a prostitute. A prostitute, of course, will demand payment. It is considered poor form, and it can be quite dangerous, not to pay a prostitute. On the other hand, of course, it is extremely poor form to offer money to a girl who is performing a sexual act because she believes herself to be "in love."

There are a few rules of thumb. If, while you are dressing, the woman in question says, "Are you goeeing to leef me a leetle geeft, m'sieur?" she is very likely a professional, and will require payment. If, on the other hand, the woman invites you to meet her parents, she is likely to be an amateur (from the Latin "amo," I love). She does not need to be paid, although she will expect a phone call.

Now, you ask, how can I get one of these amateur women to consent to all of this? What's in it for her? You might well ask. Persuading a woman that what she really wants to do with the next hour or two of her life is to submit to your sexual whims is no easy chore. The traditional technique is three-pronged: dinner, alcohol, and flattery. Talk is enormously important throughout the operation. What we call "chatting her up" is the process by which we pretend that sex is the last thing on our minds, that what we really want to do is get to know her better, discover her opinions on every possible subject, and listen to anecdotes about her family, pet dog, high school English teacher, favorite movie actor, and last boyfriend.

Your role in all of this is to nod sympathetically, mutter inanities like "You don't say" and "Well, I never," keep the drinks coming, and pay the bill. With luck, by about one in the morning, she will be drunk enough to be amenable to suggestion. She may also have one of those drunken revelations, along the lines of "Oh Christ, I've just spent the last hour talking about my stuffed animal collection, the poor bastard looks bored stiff and it cost him a fortune on food and drink, I suppose I'll have to put out." And hey presto — as long as you can get her home before she passes out, you're there!

When talking to her, it is important to make her think she's special, that you could pick her out in a crowd, that sort of thing. Women like to think they mean something to you. They don't want to think you'd go to bed with just anybody, even though most of the time it's obviously true. If you have a good memory for names, it's flattering to use hers from time to time. It is generally fatal to use the wrong name, so if you're not sure of the right name give her a pet name like Honey or Sweetheart or something equally affectionate.

Now what is it, Jackson? How much is all this going to cost? A very good question, Jackson. A professional lady will charge differing sums according to services rendered, rather like a plumber or electrician. For an act of what we used to call conventional "sexual intercourse," performed in a real bed, I should think you could expect to pay something in the vicinity of seventy-five to a hundred dollars, at the very least.

Yes, boys, that is rather a lot of money, especially on your allowance. Hence the appeal of the amateur. Let's look at the savings. Say we're dealing with a relatively unsophisticated young woman who has not yet become accustomed to the best restaurants. Well, face it, boys, a sophisticated woman is not going to take a second look at the likes of you. Let's start with the sort of young woman to whom a candle in a Chianti bottle is the *ne plus ultra* of ambience. Still, you'll want at least an adequate sort of bistro. Drinks to start with, you have the soup, she has salad, followed by the rack of lamb for her while you economize with the pasta of the day, all accompanied by a bottle of passable wine, she'll want dessert of course and at least four Spanish coffees and possibly a B-52 to clinch things. It's the drinks that always add up, especially the sorts of drinks young women like. With tax, tip, parking, and gas, you're looking at something in the range of seventy-five to a hundred dollars. At the very least.

So you see the dilemma. With the amateur, you get dinner. But you have to listen to stories about her girlfriends — who seem to lead lives of unspeakable drabness — and it's still anything but a certainty. The professional doesn't need flowers, she doesn't expect a phone call the next day, and you haven't blown a whole evening. With the professional, you still have time to do your geometry homework. And speaking of which, Jackson, what can you tell us about the isosceles triangle . . . ?

WOMEN'S LIFE PATHS

When I was just a little girl,
I asked my mother what would I be?
Will I be happy? Will I be rich?
Here's what she said to me:
Que sera, sera . . . ."
Ancient folk wisdom

Ahh, ladies' lives used to be *so* easy. They were born to be our wives and mothers. Breeding stock. Domestic appliances, with cute little button noses, with self-cleaning ovens, and no pesky options to trouble their pretty little heads, no wonder they outlived us by 10 years!

THEN

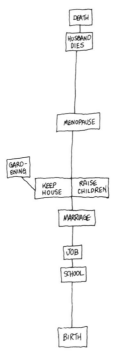

But they couldn't leave well enough alone! Oh no! They burned their bras, went on the pill, and attended night school with their hairy-legged girlfriends to study arc welding. Things aren't the same as they used to be:

NOW

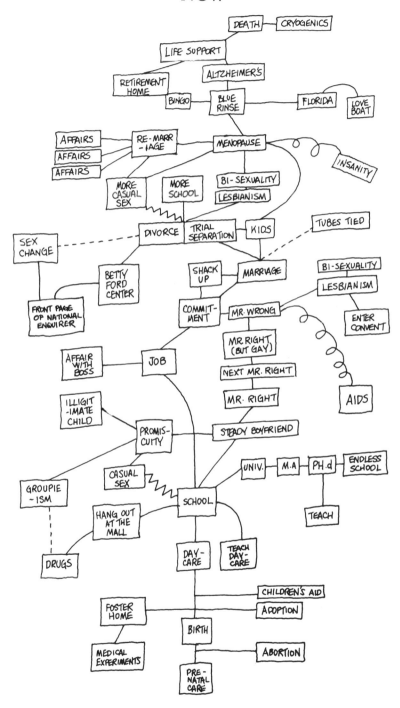

WHAT FACE SHAPE DO YOU HAVE?

Every woman's favorite leisure time activity is skimming vapid women's magazines, trying to identify their face shape from the monthly guides provided, and once identified, camouflaging the flaws and attempting to more closely resemble someone on "Dynasty." Dumb? Sure, and not half as much fun as watching the NFL all weekend, but it's low impact and there's no off-season . . . .

IDENTIFY YOUR FACE SHAPE

Oval   Triangle   Rectangle

Amoeba   Big Bird   Popeye

Jimmy Hoffa   Shit Head   Pizza

WOMEN AND FAT

Quick: name the sport in which women are better than men. Nope. Uh-uh. Wrong again. Give up? Marathon swimming. That's right. All of the great long-distance swimmers are women. When it comes to swimming across a large body of water, we can't compete with them.

And there's a legitimate, scientific reason. It has nothing to do with strength or stamina or not having sex the night before the big event. It all boils down to one three-letter word: fat. What makes women so damn pleasant and soft to hang on to is the same thing that allows them to swim the English Channel.

Now it's not something they like to talk about, but women have a layer of subcutaneous fat which we fellows do not have. Apart from making them pleasing to cuddle with on a winter night, it helps them to float in water. Men, being all muscle and bone, sink like stones before they catch as much as a glimpse of the French coast. (Some insensitive men have argued that only a woman would be stupid enough to want to swim the English Channel, particularly since the advent of the hovercraft. Besides, by the time you reach France, your passport is soaked beyond legibility.) It is this same factor that has kept men from taking up synchronized swimming. Well, that and male legs.

This layer of fat also explains in part why women can dress in slinky little outfits at parties, while men are swaddled in three-piece suits. Lacking the insulation inherent in women, we poor men feel the cold something terrible.

It is, ironically, these same slinky outfits that provoke distress in women. The question of temperature aside, the layer of subcutaneous fat is of real use to a woman only if she intends to take up marathon swimming. And, frankly, marathon swimming is at best a minority interest for modern women. Let's be blunt, most women don't feel they look their best in noseplugs and a layer of protective grease.

Most women, if the truth be known, would gratefully sign away their chances of a self-propelled crossing of the English Channel if they could part with their subcutaneous fat. After all, the English Channel — like most of the bodies of water traversed by marathon swimmers — is a vile cesspool, a sea of oil, raw sewage, and every chemical known to man. It is also unspeakably cold.

Some of the modern woman's obsession with fat is simply a product of the times. Women, as usual, blame the current craze for thinness on men — yet another slander. The women on display in men's magazines, for instance, revel in their subcutaneous fat. Women's magazines, on the other hand, offer an endless stream of cadaverous models, each bonier than the last, and it is these skeletal specimens that today's woman attempts to emulate.

It was not ever thus. In a less obsessive time, a bit of flesh was regarded as a sign of prosperity. Only the poor were thin. In the early seventeenth century — as the paintings of Peter Paul Rubens testify — a woman was not a woman without a few generous rolls of fat in the right places. It was an era when cellulite was king. One can imagine a woman of the time studying herself critically in the mirror before an evening of pleasure, and saying unhappily to her husband, "Do you think this outfit makes me look thin?" (As always, the wise husband would have the right answer: "Not a bit, my chubby cherub. Have another piece of cake.")(See **Talking to Women**.)

Men, as always, have had to adapt to the times. We've learned to come up with the right answers to questions like that, just as we've learned to live with constant talk of dieting and the threat of liposuction, a grotesque new medical procedure whereby fat is sucked out of the body by a sort of surgical vacuum cleaner. We've lived through fat women and thin women, just as we've lived with short skirts and long skirts.

As usual, we can live with it. It's the women I worry about.

WOMEN AND LOVE

We have dealt with the subject of Women and Sex. Now we come to Women and Love, which is what crops up if you want to have sex with the same woman more than three times. It is important for a woman's self-respect to believe that this ongoing sexual relationship is in fact Love. Love, after all, is what separates us from the animal kingdom. Dogs rut; humans fall in love.

(This business of "falling in love" is interesting. It suggests a dramatic event beyond one's control, and it may be related to the idea of letting oneself be plied with alcohol so as to facilitate a sexual encounter without taking the blame for it. "Oh, I was drunk." It's the ultimate diminished responsibility defense: "I didn't choose this bozo; I just fell in love with him.")

There is that magic time very early on in what women call "a relationship" when you're merely "seeing each other." This, as you will later discover, is the best of times. The sex is great, both partners are cheerful, all's right with the world. The young man in this position will imagine that nothing can ever mar his happiness. He thinks that he can continue to go on "seeing" the woman in question indefinitely. He is, of course, wrong. The fellow who has been around a bit will be aware that bliss is a short-lived thing.

From the woman's point of view, this brief moment in time is also a pleasant phenomenon. "Yes," she will announce happily to her friends, "we're 'seeing each other.' " At this point, man and woman are on largely the same wavelength. This, I must tell you, cannot last. You — the man — are happy. Therefore, almost by definition, it cannot last.

You are content beyond measure "seeing" this woman. She's cute as several bugs' ears, you enjoy her company, and the sex — as already noted — is great, and getting better. Suddenly, it all changes. Women have a very definite ceiling time on "seeing" men. They're happy to "see" you for a time, but "seeing" you is merely a stage in what is either going to be, or not be, a "relationship." And this is where the roof falls in.

There will be a sort of tension in the air. A kind of ill-defined crotchetiness. A feeling that all is somehow less than tickety-boo. She will not respond to your probing questions right away. No, she's feeling all right. No, it isn't "that time." No, things are fine at the office. Well then, what is it?

"Roger," she will finally say, her lower lip showing a firmness you have not seen before, "I just don't feel this 'relationship' is going anywhere."

You shudder. A moment ago, you had been unaware that you even had a "relationship," and now you have been told that it is "going nowhere." Anything you say now could be something you regret, which in fact is almost always the case with women (see **Talking To Women**).

What you will probably say, and will regret saying, is, "But I thought we were happy just 'seeing each other!' "

This is exactly what her friends have warned her about (see **What Women Talk About**). In their eyes, you have been leading her on, taking what you wanted, and offering nothing in return, as if those expensive dinners just paid for themselves. Your insensitivity has proven her friends correct. You are exactly the parasitic male scum they have painted you. For the woman in question, there is now no going backward. You must now either end it — proving that she and her harpy friends were right — or you must go forward into the next stage.

If you are fifteen, the next stage is "going steady." You may have to provide an inexpensive piece of jewelry or a school sweater. If you are a grown-up, the price will be far higher. You are talking here about "being in love," and that means lawyers, loan officers, credit managers, real estate agents, and her family: the five horsepersons of the modern apocalypse.

Men, fortunately, are adaptable. One can get used to "being in love," and one does. One even comes to like it sometimes, unaware that "being in love" itself is simply another stage. That's right, friend. If you think you've gone about as far as you can go, think again.

(See **Women and Marriage**.)

GREAT MOMENTS IN THE HISTORY (AND FUTURE) OF WOMANHOOD

2040 B.C. FIRST BULL DYKE. Bathsheberta refuses to take part in the chain of "begats" of Genesis. This woman refuses to bear children and concentrates on her career as an ox driver and part-time gladiator.

1400 B.C. Ruth of Peloponisia breaks with the "ass jawbone" tradition by killing 600 Sumerians with the "jawbone of a mother-in-law."

1192 A.D. A woman, "Average-sized Nell," is inducted into bandit/adventurer Robin Hood's band of Merry Men, mostly to do the cooking and cleaning. While remaining for several years in a domestic capacity, she was summarily dismissed from the Merry Men for her refusal to wear the standard Lincoln-green wardrobe, after having her "colors done" at the Nottingham Beauty Shoppe.

1222-40. THE WOMEN'S CRUSADE. Women crusaders journey to free the Holy Lands from the Heathens and their bad table manners. They get no further than Thrace, where they fall into factionalism and infighting over a meal check split 1,000 ways.

1502. POPETTE GLADYS. Gladys di Pasta, little known wife of Pope Sixtus II, forces her husband to have all cellulite textures sandblasted from the thighs of the Vatican's extensive collection of statuary.

1533. FIRST DAMSEL IN DISTRESS. Lady Marion de Montbrun, on her deathbed, admits to never having been "in distress." Her life, in fact, appears to have been pretty cosy.

1803. Phillippe de Stayfree invents the first sanitary napkin, in Cote de Kotex, France.

1804. The "COFFEE CLATCH" (das Kaffe Gabfest) is invented, Prattleburg, East Prussia.

1840. Vienna. Gynecology becomes a separate discipline. Formerly, along with dentistry, it was performed by village blacksmiths.

1852. Shower curtain rod invented 117 years before the first discovery of pantyhose.

SEPTEMBER 1907. FIRST AIRPLANE (ALMOST). East Wheetabix, Montana. The Tight sisters complete a working aircraft of their own design a full four months before the famous flight of the Wright brothers at Kittyhawk. Their claim is rendered invalid; they did not actually fly the aircraft since they felt it would, in the words of one of them, "muss our hair."

DECEMBER 21, 1935. Phil Donahue born.

JANUARY 28, 1936. Alan Alda born.

1938. FIRST WOMAN SENTENCED TO THE ELECTRIC CHAIR. Maude Sneed, electrocuted in a state penitentiary in Alabama, is the first woman executed in the electric chair. Ironically, the chair was also designed by a woman; Chippendale with mauve silk brocade.

1942. Toolbox, Wisconsin. The "eight-items or less" checkout aisle is invented at Mo's Marketeria.

1944. Iwo Jima. Scant minutes after the flag-raising episode, a bunch of WACs organized the BRIDE PARTY AT IWO JIMA.

1952. Underwire bra invented by Chilean torture technicians funded by the CIA.

1955. Detroit introduces the first automobile aimed at women: the PLYMOUTH VANITY features two rear-view mirrors, one for make-up and one for rear viewing.

JANUARY 1976. 1976 declared INTERNATIONAL WOMEN'S YEAR. To celebrate, women's rights are given a two-minute tribute at the Super Bowl half-time show.

1980. Shelley Winters makes her final (of 827) appearances on the "Merv Griffith Show," babbling about her man-loving lifestyle.

1985. HURRICANES NAMED AFTER WOMEN. August 1985. Hurricane Gidget devastates Haiti, leaving 70,000 homeless.

1988. It is confirmed by independent observers that a woman gave a Chicago cab driver $10 for a $8.25 ride and said "keep the change."

1989. THE DEFINITIVE GUIDE TO THE OPPOSITE SEX published in Montreal.

. . . AND FUTURE

1991. Despite pressures from women's groups, scientific evidence confirms once and for all that disco does indeed SUCK.

1992. The United States Forestry Service mascot, Smokey the Bear, is replaced by the feminist animal, Pussy the Cat.

AUGUST 1993. POPEYE THE SAILOR MAN successfully sued for palimony by long-time girlfriend Olive Oyl.

DECEMBER 1993. Hell's Angels Motorcycle Club drops the sexist barriers and adopts women as full members. Women are now entitled to full club privileges, including sloppy seconds at all club-sanctioned orgies.

MAY 1994. Mother Teresa's Work-Out Video goes Double Platinum.

JUNE 1994. Conceptual artist Cristo "wraps" Phil Donahue and his entire audience.

MAY 30, 1995. First woman wins INDY 500. Andrea Granitelli becomes the first woman to win the Memorial Day Classic. Celebrating afterward on Main Street Indianapolis, she is clocked by state troopers at 214 m.p.h., but let off with a warning when she bursts into tears.

1995. Jane Russell, the "full-figured gal," passes away. She weighs 340 pounds and wears a G-cup.

1996. FRIDAY THE 13TH PART XII. For the first time, the film series' psychopathetic, goalie-masked hero, "Jason," is reincarnated as a woman. The grisly murders continue, but the cadavers are found neatly wrapped and sealed in large freezer bags.

1997. Union Carbide markets a line of disposable five-day silicone breast implants "for a firmer, fuller you — no muss, no fuss."

1997. The NRA (National Rifle Association), becomes dominated by women. The organization now promotes and protects the rights of U.S. citizens to bear arms and dildoes.

1998. First cross-sex Oscar. Mervin (nee Meryl) Streep, unchallenged after her sixth Best-Actress Oscar, undergoes a sex change and wins Best-Actor Oscar for her performance in *The French Lieutenant's Buddy*.

2001. NASA's space shuttle "The Good Ship Venus," sets off for Saturn with an historic all-woman crew. The mission aborted due to bickering over the blow dryer.

2005. An international team of women scientists caps a 17-year research program by announcing it has eliminated the "static cling" problem.

2008. Birth control pill for men invented. It is inexpensive, safe, and effective. Only known side effect is a propensity to attend Tupperware parties.

2011. YOU'VE COME A LONG WAY BABY. For the first time, women surpass men in smoking-related deaths. Field Lawns Memorial Corp. institutes a new line of "Virginia Slims" longer, thinner caskets.

2014. Elizabeth T. Moore elected first female president of the United States. She immediately cancels statehood of 'sexist' Puerto Rico, appoints an ambassador to *Cosmopolitan*, commits $9 billion to "sensible shoe" research, and outlaws fishing, camping, and all forms of professional sports on television.

2020. First abortion referral clinic established on the moon (bombed by pro-life lifeforms from Jupiter in 2028).

2021. Alan Alda dies; donates his sensitivity to science.

2022. First Biological Clock Transplant recipient, Monica Burg-Honda, becomes single mother of hyperactive quints at age 68 when 19-year-old boyfriend Raoul refuses to make an honest woman of her.

2040. WET SPOT ELIMINATED. Lesbianism overtakes heterosexuality as the favored sexual orientation among female MBAs.

2089. THE KODAK "CRETINETTE," a camera so easy, even a woman can use it, is invented.

2207. After centuries of protest from women's groups, the swimsuit competition is eliminated from the Miss America Pageant. Contestants are now judged on talent, poise, beauty, and the ability to cry while wearing a tiara.

6086. Men finally figure out women.

WHAT WOMEN TALK ABOUT

The gentlemen of the Opposite Sex Women Watching Team have been working overtime to answer the age-old question of what women talk about among themselves. We have followed them everywhere, using every possible disguise and subterfuge, to get to the bottom of this. Unfortunately, our glasses steamed up in the locker room, but we were still able to eavesdrop on their conversation. And very interesting it was too.

They talk about food, both from an eating and a dieting point of view. They talk about clothes. And, yes, they talk about men. And that's when we started taking notes.

We can report that when women talk about men, it's nothing like when men talk about women. It's like two completely different species. If a man and a woman get together and make a little magic, there are two completely different ways in which their friends will respond. His male friends will say, "Haven't seen you at the pub lately. Working overtime?" Her friends will ask if they've named a date.

Men are frequently accused of kissing and telling. This is perhaps the foulest libel directed at the male sex. A man whose friend has become embroiled in a romantic situation will ask probing questions like, "How do you like the Lakers this year?" The most loaded question is likely to be, "So, you going to be able to get away for golf next week?" No one will ask if she has a belly button that goes in or out. No one will inquire whether she has good childbearing hips, or whether she's sensitive to one's needs, or if she called when she said she would, or how much she makes.

Women, on the other hand, tell all. Don't kid yourself. Within twenty-four hours of your turning up at her doorstep, most of the women she has known since high school will know your name, your income, the state of your wardrobe, your conversational skills, and damn near every detail of your sexual performance. (You may be lucky. She may be trying to impress her female friends, exaggerating your qualities to reflect well on herself. Knowing smiles from her girlfriends will confirm this.)

Women, of course, will claim that this looks good on them. This, they argue, is yet another case of their being able to discuss their feelings honestly, as if discussing one's feelings honestly is some sort of good thing. Women love to discuss their feelings, particularly during the last game of the World Series. For this reason, it is good for women to have female friends to talk with, to get this out of their system so that you can watch the game in peace.

The bad thing about women discussing their feelings is that it makes them aware of their feelings, which is seldom good news for the rest of us. It leads to conversational openings like, "Honey, I was talking to Vicky, Nicki, and Becky, and I've been thinking . . . ." And the least you're going to get away with is painting the outside of the house.

The worst thing women do together is goad one another on. They complain plenty about men. Boy, do they complain. But if one of them starts up with a new guy, the others won't quit until she's married and miserable. Say you go out for dinner with a woman. Tomorrow she'll be in contact with a whole coven of cronies, probably by conference call. Perhaps they'll get together, which is even worse, because they'll drink a few bottles of cheap Chardonnay and things will really get graphic. Your woman will mention that she went for dinner with you. Watch out.

"What's his name?"
"Is he single?"
"Do you know he's single?"
"How come he's single?"
"Something wrong with him?"
"Where's he come from?"
"You're sure he's single?"
"What's he look like?"
"Is his hair real?"
"What's he do?"
"What does it pay?"
"Thirty minimum would be my guess."
"Gotta be thirty-five, maybe forty."
"Did he pay?"
"Where did you meet him?"
"How was the food?"
"Did you have the lamb?"
"I hear the salmon's good there."
"He didn't let anything slip about a wife on the scene?"

"Any kids?"

"So what happened?"

"Your place?"

"Typical. He couldn't take you back to his place, could he?"

"I hope he brought a, you know, with him?"

"So then what — ?"

"Twice?"

"Christ!"

"On a week night?"

"What were the desserts like?"

"So how did you leave it?"

"Has he called?"

"Did he say he would?"

"They always say they will."

"They're all the same."

"So is he cute?"

"I've heard the desserts are good there."

"Was he, you know, responsive to your needs?"

"And you're sure he's single?"

"I've been there. I didn't think the desserts were that good."

"Is he a good dresser?"

"Is he good?"

"What did you wear?"

"Oh, nice."

"You look thin in that outfit."

"Is he, you know, built?"

"We need more wine!"

There will follow a detailed analysis of your physical proportions, speculation as to your long-term intentions, and a full and frank discussion about the menu at the restaurant. Before long, one of the women will wonder aloud what she'll wear at the wedding, while another, embittered by a life of disappointment, will disparage your commitment to the woman in question.

This is all absolutely true. You, by comparison, might go to the pub the next evening. A friend will ask, "So, did you watch the game last night?"

"No," you will reply, "I was out."

"Pity," your friend will observe. "Good game."

BIKINI WAXING EXPLAINED

This is a delicate subject. The less said the better.

Before

After

THREE REASONS TO BE GLAD THAT MEN DON'T SUFFER FROM PMS
(PREMENSTRUAL SYNDROME)

YOU JUST DON'T KNOW WHAT IT'S LIKE!

I CAN'T BE HELD RESPONSIBLE!

HEY; IT WAS THAT TIME OF THE MONTH!!

WOMEN AND MARRIAGE

Well, here we are. You never thought it would come to this, did you? You met this girl, you liked her, one thing followed another. Wasn't it nice?

And then it changed. Women are supposed to be such romantic creatures. We can get by on love alone. Who cares what the world says? We've got each other — who needs this little piece of paper? Well, friend, you might find yourself saying all these things, but it won't get you very far. Love is all very well, but there are larger forces at work here, and you don't stand much of a chance. The process that began with a bit of chemistry one night over a plate of rigatoni and a bottle of wine leads inexorably onward. What began with such intimacy — just you, her, and the waiter — suddenly becomes a massive public spectacle involving dozens of people you've never met.

What went wrong? Over the second bottle of wine all that time ago, the two of you began to think there was something special in the air, and you went back to her place to check it out. Two years later, on the strength of that, her second cousin gets a free dinner. How does it follow?

First of all, there is nothing you did intrinsically wrong. Don't blame yourself. There is little you could have done to change it. Well, perhaps if you hadn't called her the next day. Still, if you hadn't called, your name would have appeared prominently on the women's network Men-Who-Didn't-Call list, and you wouldn't have been able to get a date again in that town, unless you hung out at the bus station and chatted up the new arrivals.

No, it was beyond your control. Anyway, you liked her, didn't you? She was cute. She laughed at your jokes. She listened to the story about how you wrecked your knee in high school. She liked sex, for Pete's sake. So why, when everything's been going well for so long, do you suddenly have to get a license from the government? And where does her second cousin come in?

Women love weddings. That's the one thing you have to understand. Men like to drink too much, but otherwise we tend to find weddings a bit embarrassing, particularly our own. Weddings are so public. And don't you find that the groom always looks a bit of a fool? The groom is there because it's traditional to have one at a wedding; otherwise he might just as well stay home. The groom's job is to stand about and get leered at by people he might never see again, if he's lucky. His role is to turn up, looking presentable in clothes rented especially for the occasion, and do nothing that might embarrass the bride.

It is, after all, the bride's day. She is admired by all, she receives countless kitchen appliances, and she gets a nice meal as well. What could be better? And you get congratulated. People will look you up and down as if it's a sort of slave auction. People will clink their cutlery against their glasses until you stand up and kiss each other. It's pagan, is what it is. The first time you met her parents, you pretended that you couldn't even spell sex, that somehow you were spending time with their daughter because of a common interest in bowling or movies or something. Then suddenly here you are making a meal of it on demand, and her father's paying for it.

Not that sex is going to be a big part of your life from now on. What do you call a woman who likes sex? Single. The married woman has other things to occupy her now. Furniture. Drapes. Carpeting. Husband improvement schemes.

Still, look on the bright side. Statistics reveal that married men live longer than single men. Big deal. Giant tortoises live longer than either, and nobody equates the giant tortoise with a good time.

What is it that women love about marriage? We keep returning to the influence on women's lives of girlfriends. The woman who smiles at you so tenderly over the parmesan cheese is constantly aware of her status, should she run into an old chum. The often unspoken question is, "Do you have a man?" There are four possible answers.

a. No   c. I'm in love with someone
b. I'm seeing someone   d. I'm married

Answer a. actually carries the most interesting possibilities. The woman in question may be a lesbian, a nun, unlucky in love, just taking a little time off, or a believer in the new chastity cult. It's a terrific conversational gambit, but one most women would rather die than use.

Answer b. gets a sort of, "Oh, how nice" response. "Seeing" someone — as we have learned already — doesn't carry a big *cachet* among women. It shows that a woman's making an effort, but she will have to try harder.

Answer c. is far more positive. In fact, among a handful of very progressive women, c. is just about good enough.

Nevertheless, answer d. is what they're aiming for. What it means above all is that the woman in question has actually got a guy to stand up in his best clothes (or, interestingly, in rented clothes that are better than his best clothes) in front of a crowd of people that includes her second cousin and traditionally a professional religious person, and announce out loud that he's not going to screw around.

Men, of course, are not given to public statements of that sort. Even politicians invariably look shifty when they make public promises, and they're used to it. After all, it's what we fought for when we won the secret ballot.

But you can't win them all, mate. And you don't win this one either. So just be a good sport about it, smile at the stupid jokes, and don't get caught with a bridesmaid. Oh, and don't worry too much about all the promises you have to make. According to my lawyer, anything you say under duress is unlikely to hold up in a court of law. You might want to cross your fingers, though, just in case.

WHY DO WOMEN BOTHER IF MEN ARE . . . ?

Insecure	condescending	low-brow
unfeeling	unrefined	debauched
irresponsible	sloppy	cocky
irritating	indolent	conceited
uncommunicative	macho	untrustworthy
brutish	chauvinistic	unresponsive
arrogant	pompous	secretive
humiliating	callous	sybaritic
oedipal	unruly	disorganized
dirty	truculent	messy
childish	impolite	juvenile
cold	vague	boorish
hedonistic	shallow	slovenly
unfaithful	foul-mouthed	strutting
lazy	brash	superior
hairy	immoral	feral
inarticulate	churlish	gauche
have no clothes	primitive	tyrannical
sense	fatuous	profane
uninquisitive	hedonistic	born-in-a-barn
bowlers	indifferent	irreverent
unreasonable	thick-skinned	undiplomatic
non-commital	unkempt	defiant

unobservant
thoughtless
demeaning
horny
aggressive
rough
unfeeling
inert
infantile
base
womanizing
self-centered
philandering
rakish
profligate
stubbly
dispassionate
bullshitters
libertine
self-indulgent
unemotional

obnoxious
libertine
degenerate
loutish
big
filthy
wanton
uncultured
lax
remiss
lecherous
hungry
carnal
undiscerning
libidinous
oafish
rude
messy
egotistical
uncouth
secretive

patronizing
immature
sullen
unsympathetic
undemonstrative
self-important
brazen
overbearing
chest-beating
slothful
ill-mannered
vulgar
two-timing
three-timing
disparaging
rowdy
careless
supercillious
obdurate
dissolute

WHY DO WOMEN PUT UP WITH THEM?

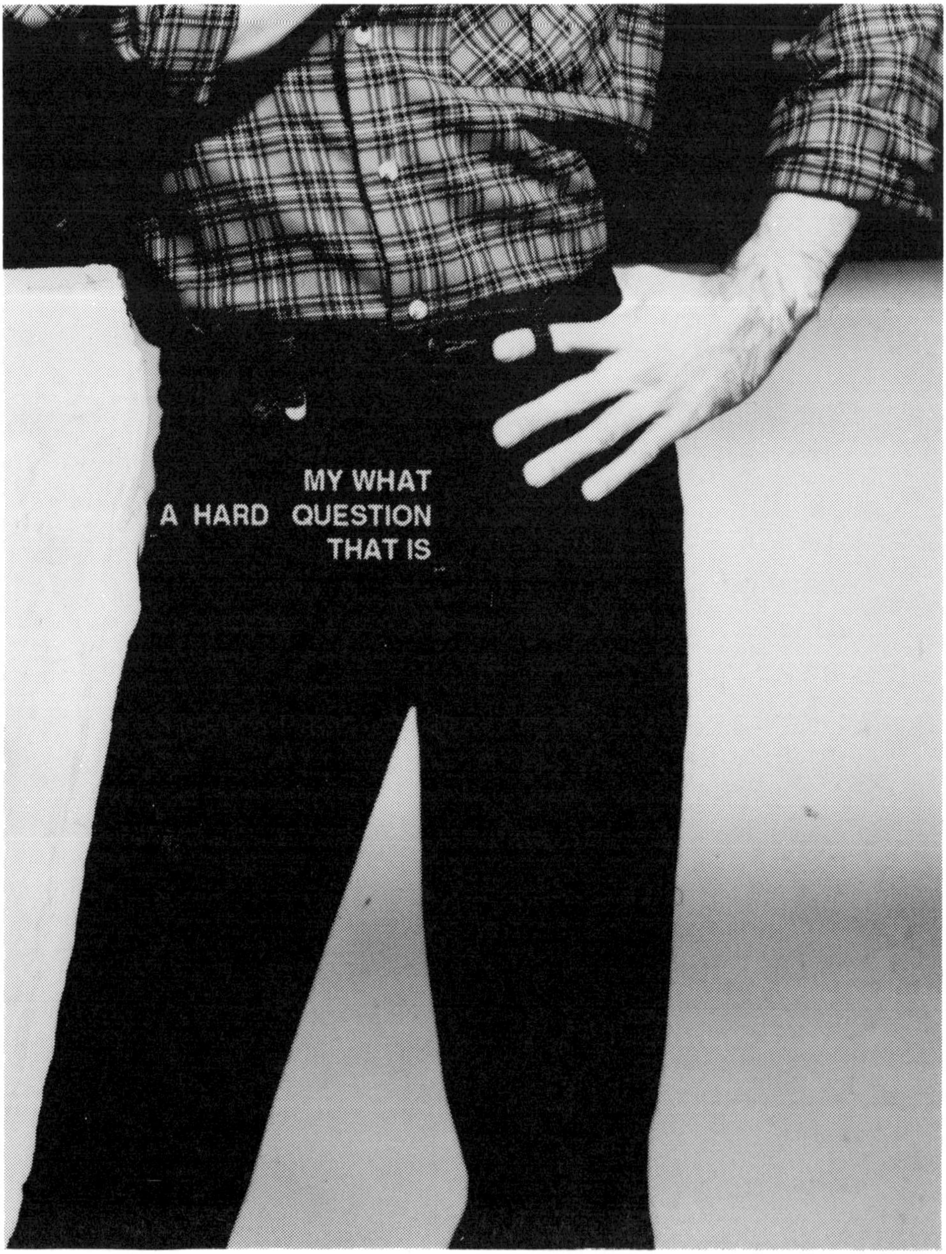
MY WHAT
A HARD QUESTION
THAT IS

TALKING TO WOMEN

Talking to women is not as simple as it sounds. Talking to women, for instance, is nothing at all like talking to men. Talking to men is a perfectly natural process, a wonderful exchange of ideas expressed without spite or ulterior motives. No one is going to steam off in a huff as the result of an all-male conversation. Oh, voices may be raised, weapons may be discharged, but there will be no hard feelings the next day. Not among the survivors, at any rate.

A man doesn't return home from an evening at the pub in tears, saying "Nobody noticed my shoes, Harvey thought my new shirt makes me look fat, and Brian made a comment about my hair!" Women will dismiss this argument as further evidence that men can't discuss their feelings, which is not entirely true. Men have strong feelings about — to cite just one example — the designated hitter rule, and are prepared to discuss it endlessly. I might call you a horse's ass for your defense of the designated hitter rule; you might call me a sloppy-minded hobbledehoy for my churlish opposition to the rule; I might then call . . . well, you get the picture.

Does this exchange lead to an irreversible rupture in our "relationship?" Does this mean we shall never again sit together at the bar, that our mutual friends will have to choose sides, that we can never again borrow each other's crosscut saw or Quik-Mo electric lawnmower with automatic mulcher? Of course not! Don't be absurd! Why, within five minutes of exhausting the designated hitter rule debate, we shall more than likely be sitting together, arms linked, singing the old songs.

Talking to a woman is, by comparison, a minefield, particularly if the woman in question is one whom you are "seeing," or "in love" with, or, even worse, "married" to. One false move, and you're in deep trouble. The shortage of women philosophers is not, I think, an accident. Women are not gifted with an ability to see the larger picture, to approach a subject with objectivity. If you, for example, suggest — in an entirely theoretical way — that monogamy might not be the absolute ideal for all men, she will break into tears, certain that you are having an affair.

Avoid the theoretical. Women don't like it, and they will think you are getting at them somehow. Be careful with irony. Irony can be all too easily misinterpreted. Be moderate in expression — except in praise — at least until you see how the land lies. Be vague whenever possible, especially when answering questions.

There are certain subjects that require enormous care. Possibly the greatest of these is weight — usually hers, not yours. The question "Do you think I'm getting fat?" can be answered in two ways: a. Not a bit, and b. Good Lord, no, if anything I've been worried about you fading away! Answer a. is too weak, and may lead to an hour of subsequent interrogation until you finally come across answer b. Even answer b. is likely to be followed by "Now, I want you to be completely honest."

"I want you to be completely honest" is one of a woman's most loaded statements. "I want you to be completely honest" takes no prisoners. It is indeed the dum-dum bullet in her arsenal. This is the time for a man to put down his newspaper and pay attention, hoping he can remember the original question. This is no time for flippancy. You're in the big leagues now, son. The correct response to "I want you to be completely honest" is to tell her exactly what she wants to hear.

(The age-old complaint that men cannot discuss their feelings honestly is false. Men can discuss their feelings as honestly as you like; they have simply learned the hazards of doing so.)

The variation on "Do you think I'm getting fat?" is "Do you think I look fat *in this outfit?*" This is a tricky one. There may be a temptation to take the affirmative and pin the rap on the offending outfit, especially if it's a new one and can still be taken back to the store for a refund, but the temptation should be resisted. There should be no suggestion of fat in anything you do or say. The worst thing you can say to any of the fat questions is, "Aw shucks, honey, I'd love you no matter how fat you get."

Talking with women requires the utmost discretion, whatever the subject. Women are aware of the widespread belief that they become like their mothers, so don't criticize her mother. She has probably read a magazine article that pointed out that she married you because you remind her of her father, so don't criticize her father. In short, don't criticize anybody or anything. Make jokes when you can, but never sound flippant. Follow these rules and you'll be fine. Maybe.

MS. GOOSE: NON-SEXIST NURSERY RHYMES

Remember innocent youth? The halcyon preliberated days of "you show me yours and I'll show you mine" before we even thought of wrapping them both in latex and spermacidal jelly? Remember when we sat on daddy's knee and read timeless nursery rhymes and fairy tales written by sexist monsters like the Brothers Grimm and Hans Christian Andersen? That's a thing of the past; daddy's on his knees now, scrubbing out the oven, while mommy is off interfacing with limpwristed brokers. Feminism's progesterone-fueled crusade to seek out, shrilly condemn, and rewrite in its own egalitarian image perceived chauvinism in all facets of life will stop at nothing. Mother Goose is a dead duck. She's fair, but she's foul.

Mary had a little lamb,
It's fleece was white as snow.
And everywhere that Mary went
Sexist creeps and perverts
Came on to both of them.

Little Bo Peep lost her virginity,
And didn't know where to find it.
Took maternity leave at home,
Raised her lovechild alone.
And to a fully-funded daycare
consigned it.

Three male mice, three male mice,
See how they run, see how they run,
They all ran after the farmer's wife,
She cut off their testicles with a carving knife,
Did you ever see such a sight in your
life,
As three _____ mice?

There was an old woman,
Who lived in a sensible shoe.
She had 1.8 children
And held down a responsible job in
senior management at a computer
software company.

Jack Sprat could eat no fat,
His Ex was real mean,
And what her lawyers did to him,
It really was obscene!

Diddle diddle dumpling,
My boyfriend John
Went to bed with a condom on
Pill, IUD, spermacidal jell,
Diddle diddle dumpling
Biology is hell!

Old Mother Hubbard,
Went to the cupboard
To get her poor dog a bone.
When she got there,
The cupboard was bare,
So she got her MBA and started a profitable meat-packing concern.

Peter, Peter, Pumpkin eater,
Had a wife and couldn't keep her
So she dumped the useless jerk
Hit him with alimony and a garnishee at work!

Georgie Porgie pudding in pie,
Kissed the girls and made them cry.
The ones he kissed took him to court,
Filed for rape and child support.

Rub-a-dub-dub, three gals in a tub,
And you know how they got there, don't you?
The butcher, the baker,
The candlestick maker,
All enjoyed the boost from affirmative action, I'll betcha

Humpty Dumpty sat on a wall
Humpty Dumpty had a great fall
All the Queen's women
And all the Queen's dykes
Made a simply scrumptuous souffle

Ba ba little girl,
Have you any choice?
Yes ma'am, yes ma'am
To raise feminism's voice.
Men will not be master,
Don't call me dame,
I want to *be* the little boy
Who lives down the lane!

Eeenie, meenie, miney mo
Catch a chauvist by the toe
If he hollers, castrate him!

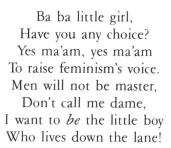

Little Ms. Muffet,
Sat on the board of directors,
Eating her curds and whey,
Along came a spider
Who sat down beside her
So she maced the creep and trans-
ferred him to the Anchorage office.

LADIES' NOBEL PRIZES

It's not fair! Every year when the Nobel Prizes are awarded in Stockholm, the Nobel laureates are yet another group of men; eminent, distinguished, outstanding in their fields of endeavor, but men all the same.

Women are not forced to compete with men in a variety of pursuits and pastimes; ice hockey, basketball, four-man luge, even the Academy Awards. We don't make them compete in the Miss Universe Pageant, do we? Why should women be brow-beaten into competing in fields where biology and societal repression put them at a natural disadvantage? Let's face it; physics, chemistry, medicine, literature, peace — these are men's things. Nothing for women to worry their pretty little heads about. The Nobel Prize categories are limited, sexist, and *just too hard!*

In recognition of this, we would like to propose establishing the Ladies' Nobel Prizes — to honor and encourage excellence in fields where women naturally excel.

1991 NOBEL PRIZE WINNING WOMEN:
Nobel laureattes gather in Stockholm to receive their prizes!
L. to R.: Maimie Updike (USA), EMPATHY; Patricia H. Anderson (Canada), COSMETOLOGY; Heidi Kneebent (Austria), INTUITION; Adolpha Eichmann (Argentina), TASTE; Adriana (Mom) Hititoff (USSR) MATCHMAKING.

WHAT DO WOMEN KNOW?

And Why Are They Such Know-It-Alls?

There are men who maintain that women know absolutely nothing worth knowing. How many women can tell you, in succinct but thorough terms, the principles of nuclear fission? They couldn't tell you the 1973 American League MVP or explain the infield fly rule. And if you showed them the crankcase from a Buick LeSabre and asked them to identify it and describe its function, they'd just do that cute pouting thing they do, stamp their little feet, and say it was stuff that wasn't worth knowing. They'd say you weren't being fair.

But to say they know nothing of consequence is perhaps not entirely accurate. Women themselves would argue that in fact they know damn near everything there is to know. While this argument is, of course, laughable, it might be worth examining just what exactly women do know. You might be surprised.

For beginners, women know a remarkable amount of quite practical stuff. Women, for example, know the difference between baking soda and baking powder, a secret known to only half a dozen men currently living. Women also know how to remove a cranberry sauce stain from a dress that's 80% wool, 20% some not especially natural product that evolved from the U.S. space program. Women can distinguish endive from arugula, and they can tell you exactly how many calories lurk in any remotely edible substance.

A woman knows how to change a typewriter ribbon without getting ink all over her pretty hands. She knows your birthday, your mother's birthday, the birthdays of all members of your immediate family as well as those of everyone she works with. She also knows your anniversary, which is probably more than you do.

A woman knows if you've been drinking at lunchtime, even if you've chewed a mint afterwards. She knows — from doing the quizzes in *Cosmo* — whether you're having an affair with the blonde tramp in the marketing department. Probably from the same source, she knows what kind of person you are from the shoes you're wearing, even if she picked them out herself.

Most important, a woman knows what's best for you, whatever foolish notions you might have. (If the woman in question is Margaret Thatcher, she knows what's best for the entire human race, and woe to anyone who dares to disagree. If you think the woman in your life is a know-it-all, just imagine how Denis Thatcher feels.) A woman knows what foods are good for you, and when you've had enough to drink. She knows when you've told the same story twice in one evening.

A woman knows where you've gone wrong. She knows what you might have become had she got her hands on you earlier and if you hadn't been so stubborn in resisting her. Finally, she knows if you've been bad or good — but you're going to pay for it anyway.

WOMEN'S UNDER-SHIRT BRA-REMOVAL SECRET REVEALED

For centuries men have spent sleepless nights wondering how women can do it. You know, taking off their bras without first taking off their shirts! Men have died attempting to remove their underwear without first removing their outer garment. Houdini tried and failed! But women do it all the time and are oh so smug about it. It has been a closely guarded secret, passed down from sister to sister through the ages. Here, for the first time, anywhere, exclusively, we reveal, step by astonishing step, the secret!

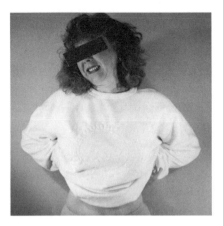

Unfasten bra

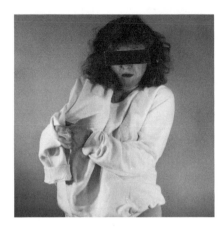

Remove one arm

Slide bra off that arm

Reach in opposite sleeve

Whip bra out through the sleeve

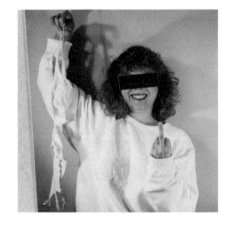

PROFESSIONAL RESEARCHER
MEN, DO NOT TRY THIS WITHOUT
PROPER MEDICAL SUPERVISION!

Our researcher continues to work
on the puzzle of men's
non-disrobing underwear removal

67

WOMEN'S CONTRIBUTION TO SCIENCE

Like the list of Italian war heroes, any guide to women's contribution to the field of science is necessarily short. Basically, there ain't much; Madame Curie and Typhoid Mary. After that, it's a lot of head scratching and foot shuffling, and padding the list with transvestite male scientists.

Discussing the scientific and technological inventiveness of the female brain is like discussing the marksmanship of a fish with a machine gun.

WOMEN'S INVENTIONS	MEN'S INVENTION'S
poodle sweaters	the wheel
little suitcase wheels	fire
drink umbrellas	shopping malls
sofa slip-covers	insulin
jello molds shaped like fish	Lamborghini Contach
L'Eggs pantyhose cartons	radar
nonalcoholic beer	electron microscope
thank you cards	Valium
bathtub pillows	television
	TV Guide
	baseball
	polio vaccine
	ballpoint pen
	nine iron
	landscaping
	flourescent lighting
	laser beams
	ice cube tray
	nuclear fission
	black velvet paintings
	Indy 500
	gun powder
	fibre optics
	Elvis mirrors
	Etch-A-Sketch

THE SEX OBJECT CONTROVERSY

Men and women will never really understand each other. Women spend staggering sums of money to look attractive. They buy glossy magazines, they buy clothes, they buy stuff to put on their faces, they buy over-priced perfumes to smell good, they pay untold sums to have their hair done. They go on diets that resemble hunger strikes, they spend hours at aerobics classes, some of them even lift weights. All to look great.

And it works. They look terrific. But, having gone to all this trouble and expense, what happens when they go out in public? Some guy — it could be you, it could be me — will notice this vision of loveliness, and as a simple gesture of appreciation will cry out, "O-o-o-o-oh babeeeee!!! Come to papa!!!"

Now, you would think that the woman in question would glow with pleasure at having provoked exactly the sort of response she has spent money and time to encourage. She looks like a million bucks, and well she might. She cries out to be admired. But just you try to admire her, and what do you get? "Buzz off, buster!"

If pressed, a woman will tell you that she doesn't want to be treated as a sex object. As if, after all her exertions, we are supposed to lower our car window and praise her analytical faculties.

And here's the crunch. The problem, way down deep inside, is that men can't really understand what's so wrong with being a sex object. The average man would love to be a sex object. Women ask us how we'd like it if we couldn't walk down the street without getting whistled at and taunted by sex-obsessed women. What we say is, when do we start?

Imagine. You're trying to get to work. On the subway, women press up against you and fondle your body. Then you're walking along the street and women start yelling stuff at you, like "Come over here, big boy!" and "Oh, you big gorgeous stud!" and "Aw, don't be shy, honey — I know what you need!" Well, just how bad can it be? We'd never get much work done, but life's seldom perfect.

We issue this challenge to women. Go ahead. Show us how awful it is to be treated like a sex object. We're willing to learn. And maybe — just maybe — if you can convince us that it's really terrible, then we'll stop. OK? The challenge begins . . . Now!!

10 CAN'T-MISS LINES TO USE ON WOMEN

"Oh baby! Sit down, I think I love you!"

"Excuse me — I'm sure you've been asked this a million times, but do you know you look exactly like Christie Brinkley?"

"Hi, I'm new in town, and I've heard this is one dull, unfriendly place. Care to prove the critics wrong?"

"You've probably heard this before, but my wife doesn't understand me. No, she really doesn't. Anyway, we have an open marriage."

"Heck, I wouldn't blame you if you didn't want to talk to me. I'm feeling a little down tonight, that's all. My adorable little puppy dog got killed this morning. My chauffeur ran him over in the Rolls."

"Listen, I'm not coming on to you or anything. Tell you the truth, I've been burned once too often. I'm just not convinced a woman is capable of being gentle and caring any more."

"Actually, I'm a little reluctant to tell you what I do. People tend to go kind of crazy when I say I'm a Hollywood movie producer. I'd lie about it, but I'm incapable of lying to beautiful women."

"Hi, baby, how are — oh, God, I'm sorry, I thought you were somebody else. No, really, I'm Sean Penn's manager, and you look a lot like Madonna from this angle. Please forgive me."

"Excuse me, miss, I wonder if you could help me order a drink. You see, I've been in a monastery since I was sixteen and, well, I inherited rather a large sum of money, so I just left the monastery this afternoon and I'm afraid I don't know anything about how to go on in the real world."

"Hey, don't get me wrong. I'm not like all the other men. Tell you the truth, I'm a real feminist myself, I really am."

71

MR. RIGHT
WHAT EVERY WOMAN WANTS IN A MAN

Alan Alda's Brain

Mel Gibson's Face

Woody Allen's Sense of Humor

Mick Jagger's Lips

Sylvester Stallone's Torso

Stevie Wonder's Hands

Steven Spielberg's Wallet

Secretariat's Genitalia

Lee Iaccoca's Job

Tom Jones' Wardrobe (and libido)

THE DEFINITIVE GUIDE
to the
OPPOSITE SEX
A Women's Guide to Men

by Barbara Butch and Marjorie Thatcher

Eden Press

The Definitive Guide to the Opposite Sex

ISBN: 1-55045-010-7

© Pacquet De L'Editeur Eden

Cover cartoon: Susan Dewar
Cover design: Pamela Chichinskas & Lynette Stokes
Inside page design: Pamela Chichinskas & Lynette Stokes
Car-Masutra model: Michael Bailey

Printed in Canada at Metropole Litho
Depot légal — premier trimestre 1989
Bibliothèque nationale du Quebec

Eden Press
31A Westminster Avenue
Montreal, Quebec H4X 1Y8

Canadian Cataloguing in Publication Data

Main entry under title:
    The Definitive guide to the opposite sex

Is comprised of two publications, back to back:
    A Woman's guide to men / by Pamela
    Chichinskas and Lynette Stokes; A Man's guide
    to women / by Tony Jenkins and Nicholas Pashley.
ISBN 1-55045-010-7

1. Sex role--Humor.   2. Men--Humor.   3. Women--
Humor.   4. Interpersonal relationships--Humor.
I. Chichinskas, Pamela   II. Stokes, Lynette
III. Jenkins, Anthony   IV. Pashley, Nicholas
IV. Title: A Woman's guide to men. V. Title:
A Man's guide to women.

PN6231.S54D44 1989   818'.5402'08   C89-090090-6

"What vain , unnecessary things are men.
How well we do without them."
Earl of Rochester, 1660

"How true, how true."
The Definitive Guide, 1990

TABLE OF CONTENTS

INTRODUCTION
7

MEN AND THEIR HEROES
9

THE TOP 15 SEXIST VALUE JUDGMENTS
14

THE RELATIONSHIP
BETWEEN MEN AND SPORTS
15

YOUNG MALE PROFESSIONAL
CASH FLOW CHART
20

MEN AT THE TOP
21

GADGET JUNKIES
25

THE CAR-MASUTRA
MALE DRIVING POSITIONS
29

MALE STEREOTYPES
RICH MAN, POOR MAN, PLAYBOY, GEEK
33

SELF-IMAGE
A MAN'S MOST IMPORTANT ASSET
36

THE HISTORY HALL OF SHAME
40

WHY DO MEN THINK WE LIKE IT WHEN
44

THE PENILE COLONY
44

MALE JEOPARDY
45

LOW BRAU BEER
46

BETE-A-TETE
47

NOT THE MARRYING KIND
49

7 QUESTIONS ABOUT MEN
THAT WOMEN CAN'T ANSWER
55

WHEN HE SAYS HE REALLY MEANS
55

SEX IN THE 1990s
56

TAPPING THE MOTHER LOAD
60

HOW TO DEKE OUT MEN
64

THE COMMUNICATION GAP
66

THE SEVEN STAGES OF MAN
69

THE IDEAL WOMAN
72

INTRODUCTION

Of all the complaints that women have about men, "I just don't understand them" is the least frequent. Unlike Freud, no female voice has been heard to cry in desperation, "What *is* it that men want?" On the contrary, we know the answer all too well. Men simply lack the mystery of the oppressed.

Because men have taken all the credit for building our civilizations, while recording their achievements in our history books, we have had access to only one version of the truth: the gospel according to man. Indeed, men have always confused their side of the story with the truth.

So it's no wonder they don't understand women. They jeer at the notion of woman's intuition, and they roll their eyes when we color-match our make-up with our clothing. Men are not subtle creatures.

Over the years women have found men's lack of self-knowledge and insensitivity truly frightening, especially considering that men have the power to control women's destiny. And don't let them kid you; there is no *war between the sexes*. The relationship between men and women has been that of master and slave for centuries.

So why do women put up with them? Because we are compassionate, because we are incorrigible optimists; and because *someone* has to notice when they run out of ketchup.

This guide is for all women over the age of twenty-one who need to take blood pressure medicine because of the men in their lives, as well as for those young innocents who have yet to play second fiddle to Saturday night sports, and cope with the myriad expressions of male angst. And it is a sensible alternative to watching Woody Allen movies.

For all members of the opposite sex out there, perhaps reading our side of *The Definitive Guide* will help you realize that — no matter how much you'd like to kid yourself— women have got your number. So when you come to the bit about you, take it like a man.

MEN AND THEIR HEROES

If ever there was a man unable to come to terms with his relationships, Hamlet was that guy. He didn't like his mother, he neglected his girlfriend, he knocked off his uncle, and was obsessive about his father. And sex? The man could think of nothing else. When he wasn't having lurid thoughts about his mother's second marriage, he was getting his jollies imagining his girlfriend in a nun's outfit. He spent most of his time dragging himself around the palace hinting about his intentions and striking the occasional pose. And the rest of the time it was whine, whine, whine, whine.

Don't take my word for it; go ahead and read the play, if you've got a few free hours and a large bottle of sherry close at hand. And you know what? You'll discover that Hamlet's exactly the kind of self-indulgent, self-interested, and self-destructive jerk that men love to make heroes out of.

The fact is that if you bother to examine male heroes closely enough, you will discover that the kind of hero your man chooses will give you previously unhoped for — and perhaps unwished for — insight into this crude creature's soul.

Male heroes can be broken down into five basic types; men who are tough and slick with women, men who are tough and slick with other men, tragic heroes (men who have failed to be as tough and slick as they deserved to be), men who are tough and slick with bats and balls, and men who are too tough and slick to be categorized.

If you've noticed a consistent theme running through these types, award yourself a silk-lined cast iron facsimile of a jock strap, because you're right. Yes, all male heroes are as hard as nails and as smooth as butter, and it is to this condition that their more earthly counterparts aspire — if only in their dreams.

MEN WHO ARE TOUGH AND SLICK WITH WOMEN

There is, of course, no such animal outside men's fantasies, and the occasional John Wayne movie. Most men have not yet caught on to the fact that women are not looking for a man with true grit; they've had just about as much grit as they can take over the last 2,000 years or so. But men will persist in dreaming of themselves spouting a few glib but clever lines, then having their way with the thrilled and willing heroine up against the nearest wall.

Reality — in the form of a swift kick in their heroic proportions — would soon cure these poor deluded hero-worshippers were they to try to live the dream.

Heroes of this kind include James Bond (all five portrayals), Clint (go ahead make my fantasy) Eastwood, Burt Reynolds (*with* hairpiece), and, more recently, Superman — now that he's banished rumors by getting himself a girlfriend.

MEN WHO ARE TOUGH AND SLICK WITH OTHER MEN

Welcome to the cowards' gallery — and a really sorry crowd of admirers they are. They would love to be super-tough, but they're

afraid their wife might complain. Instead, they grimace at themselves in the mirror while shaving, and, on days when they're feeling extra tough, they answer the budgie bird back.

In reality, these sad creatures are better suited to being the recipients of violent acts than the perpetrators. And yet, for some reason beyond the understanding of all women, these masochists think that it's noble to be the kind of man who can successfully endure four days of Chinese water torture. It does not occur to them that it is smarter to run away.

Their heroes include Sly Stallone, John Wayne, Arnold Schwartzenegger (even though his marriage into the Kennedy family has given rise to suspicions that he might be either smart or a social climber), and Chuck Norris (whom everyone can comfortably assume is neither).

TRAGIC HEROES WHO DESERVED TO BE TOUGHER AND SLICKER

It is with this category that the most dangerous of the opposite sex identify. It is the resting place for heroes who failed to live up to their true

potential because something or someone — generally alcohol or women — brought them down. This is where the admirers of Hamlet live. Such equal mixtures of ego and self-pity are perfectly suited to the male ethos.

Heroes are Macbeth (who might have made it big had it not been for his grasping wife), Dylan Thomas (who could have been one of the all-time literary greats had it not been for booze — administered to him by *his* grasping wife), and Richard Nixon (who could have been re-elected if it hadn't been for the law).

MEN WHO ARE TOUGH AND SLICK WITH BATS AND BALLS

These sports demigods are the only real male heroes for whom men are willing to be groupies. They worship the ground that these heroes work-out on. Sports devotees will call their hero's name forlornly from the stands at baseball games, they'll crowd an auditorium to watch two men beat each other up on a ten by ten screen, and they'll shout "good check" when their favorite defenseman leaves a trail of blood behind him on the ice.

They are blind in their praise. Ask any man, "Who d'you think's done more for culture in America, Itzak Perlman or Dave Winfield?" And he'll reply, "Perlman? Remind me. What are his stats?"

Superheroes in this category include Wayne Gretzky, Pete Rose, and Mean Joe Green (contrary to all male assertions about violence in sports, meanness is a must if you want to really endure). Like Yogi Bera's, these men's names will live on when Bach, Einstein, and Pasteur are long forgotten.

MEN WHO ARE TOO COOL TO BE CATEGORIZED

This is a small but elite category, characterized by rock and roll performers and men who have more money than they know what to do with.

It is a statistical fact that, from the time they reach puberty until their mid-fifties — and sometimes later — a large percentage of North American males are convinced that they are going to be rock and roll stars. Having the kind of person who makes the grade in this profession persistently rammed down their throats on MTV gives rise to this unhappy delusion.

Farm workers think that they can twang as well as Willie Nelson (and in this they are probably right), men who've recently had vocal chord polyps removed discover that they can still sing along with Leonard Cohen albums, and — for those who feel a need to dress up like chickens — Elton John is an admirable example to live by.

Kudos in this category to the likes of Steven Spielberg (for his money not his movies), Sting (for being able to combine the raucousness of rock music with the pretentiousness of the *artiste*), and Elvis Presley (this man was so cool that millions refuse to believe that he has been vulgar enough to die). James Joyce gets a special mention in this category for having written works that are so slick and cool as to be impenetrable. Only a man could have done it.

THE TOP FIFTEEN SEXIST VALUE JUDGEMENTS

COMPLIMENTS TO MEN	INSULTS TO WOMEN
He's playing the field	She's a slut
He's dynamic	She's pushy
He's sensitive	She's emotional
He's spontaneous	She has no self-control
He's networking	She's a gossip
He's macho	She's butch
He's laid back	She's lazy
He's preoccupied	She's dizzy
He's under stress	She has PMS
He's detached	She's frigid
He's wise	She's a know-it-all
He works out	She's a fitness freak
His face has character	She's a dog
He's wild 'n' crazy	She's hysterical
He's a party animal	She's a lush

THE RELATIONSHIP BETWEEN MEN AND SPORTS

The only thing that comes between a man and his preferred sport is his beer can.

Why are so many men such dedicated sports fans, spending great chunks of their lives watching professional male athletes play rough and tumble games while they themselves only risk beer bellies, jock itch, and hemorrhoids?

Game after game men will sprawl on their livingroom couches staring at the tube, or sit on barstools with the boys listening to the play-by-play, or sometimes even fork over the price of admission to the stadium to share in the excitement of a hometown game.

Baseball season begets football season begets hockey and basketball season — not to mention the PGA tour, car racing, skiing, and championship bowling. Sport after sport, season after season, game after game, the male jock never tires of witnessing a completed pass, a cross-check, or a pitcher scratch his crotch and spit.

Men would have women believe that sports really are *that* interesting, exciting, and entertaining. Bull feathers! The real reason jocks yell "go" and "alright" at their TV screens year after year is that they are vicariously participating in sports' masculinity sweepstakes — sometimes known as the "my dick's bigger than your dick" rating contest.

Of course they also enjoy drinking beer, the cheerleaders, and wearing baseball caps with cute little emblems on the front. But the thing that they enjoy the most is the fact that women — apart from the cheerleaders — cannot compete, and men revel in this all-male, almighty, all-American pastime — professional sports.

All sports are based on rivalry and men live for competition. Men are not capable of enjoying the playing of a game for its own sake. They are only interested in *who* won, not how. If men are forced by circumstance to miss a game (undoubtedly because of some female plot like Christmas or a family death), he will only want three questions answered: Who won? What was the final score? Were there any good fights?

This is another reason why sports are so appealing to men; sports are simple. There is a winner and a loser; no grey areas here. Men prefer their lives simple; they try to avoid complexities of any type. A single man will get up in the morning, eat breakfast, go to work, work like hell, go home, have supper, and go to bed. A married man has to get up, have a discussion with his wife, go to work, work like hell, come home, have a discussion with his wife, eat supper, go to bed. A life far too complicated for the average male.

Although men will sometimes inject some subtlety into their thinking about their preferred sport, it is often simply a reflection of the fact that, by gosh, after a six-pack of Coors, they empathize with the losing team's spirit. Witness comments such as "They played their hearts out," or "You can't take anything away from the other team." This is merely the booze talking. A product of their drunken camaraderie which they will not remember in the morning.

Sports represent other traits that are considered valuable to the truly masculine. Athletes are men's men; they have strength, ability, speed, they perform well under

pressure and constantly risk physical injury. They also make three million dollars a year, half of which is earned by selling Toyotas and underarm deodorant at half-time. After all, the game's not over until Kareem Abdul-Jabbar sells you something.

And the thing they are usually trying to sell you is beer. Beer is to men and sports as bear is to the woods — and it smells just about the same as well. The generic beer commerical would have several well-known, has-been sports stars in a bar drinking beer, watching sports on a wide-screen TV, discussing beer and sports. These commercials are almost as interesting as the games themselves.

All men understand and identify with the masculine athletic ideal. Jocks get caught up in watching sports, as if the masculinity of the athletes might rub off onto the spectators; and by being such supportive fans, they can actually become *real men*.

What 32-year-old man has given up his secret hope that he will, one day, play shortstop and win the world series for the Mets, or the Cardinals, or the Blue Jays? There on the playing field for all the world to see, he will prove that *he* is a *man*.

This is the reason why women will never be allowed to participate in men's competitive sports. The presence of women would negate the real reason for sports — the masculinity sweepstakes. How could a man prove he is more masculine and has a bigger dick if his competitor doesn't have, or indeed want, one? It wouldn't prove anything about his masculinity so why bother?

There is yet another reason why sports are so popular with men. Sports is virtually the only topic men feel comfortable with when forced to make small talk with other men. It cuts through social, economic, cultural, and racial barriers. The company's CEO feels perfectly comfortable discussing the merits of Dwight Gooden's curveball with the mailboy.

There is no such universal subject for women. A young woman meeting her prospective mother-in-law for the first time doesn't begin a conversation with "Hey, what about that eggnog?" or "Aren't those Pampers something?" But young men in similar circumstances feel perfectly secure inquiring "Hey, how about those Lakers, eh?"

Furthermore, when men talk about sports to other men they feel that it allows them to show strong emotional feelings that they wouldn't ordinarily exhibit — especially publicly.

Skeptical? Consider this example. A woman (Karen) and her husband (Ed) meet for lunch at a downtown restaurant.

Karen: "Guess what? I just got that promotion I've been expecting. Meet the new Director of Marketing."

Ed: "That's terrific honey. Congratulations."

Karen: "My new salary is $75,000 a year. Isn't that great? We can buy that new sailboat we've been dreaming about and send your mother to live in Florida."

Ed: "And I'll help you find some tax shelters dear." Then Larry, a client of Ed's, drops by their table to say hello.

Larry: "Did you see the game last night?"

Ed: "What a night! What a game! And what about Johnson's touchdown? I've never seen anything like it before. I was so excited, I screamed so loudly that I lost my voice."

Larry: "Yeah, it was really something — one for the record books. Gotta' run, catch you later."

(As Larry turns to walk away, Ed whacks him on the behind, Larry turns and punches Ed in the arm.)

Ed: "Now, what were you saying dear?"

Karen: "I don't believe this — you get ten times more excited about a stupid football game than you do about my promotion, our new income and your mother living 3,000 miles away!"

Ed:"Don't be silly dear. You're overreacting."

Nothing like a stimulating conversation about his obsession with sports to make you feel as if you're the one on steroids.

Another annoying fact about men and sports is the terminology used by jocks, athletes, sportscasters, beer ads, and even Spuds Mackenzie. Football, hockey, and baseball all require special linguistic knowledge.

Especially for understanding any televised interviews with a player or a coach. Sometimes it helps to know beforehand whether the player is merely brain-damaged or is indeed brain-dead, but this doesn't seem to make much of a difference. Neither does any inside knowledge about an athlete's cocaine habit or steroid use. The only time an athlete is lucid is when he's trying to sell you something.

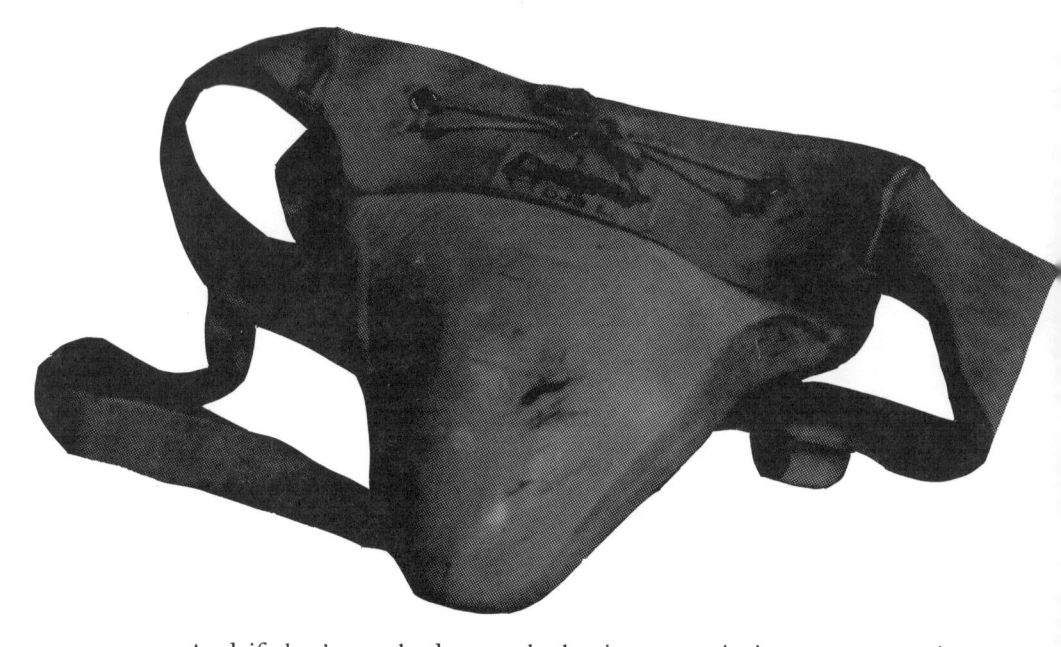

And if that's not bad enough, businessmen insist on transporting sports terminology to their everyday corporate life, thereby excluding women once again. For example, a corporate manager is a "quarterback," or a male boss will suggest "let's toss around a few ideas," a new branch plant is referred to as "an expansion ball club," or when things are really tough, they will bring in their "pinch hitter." It is almost guaranteed that this hitter doesn't wear panty hose and lipstick and drive a pink corvette — unless of course, he's an ex-quarterback for the Rams that has recently come out of the closet.

In fact, the only time women come into the lingo at all is when *he* has an "Alice" working for him. Yeah, that's right, "Alice" is an inept fool who can't shoot straight.

There is only one thing that women can learn from the relationship between men and sports. And it isn't that old adage "It's not whether you win or lose, it's how you play the game." No, no man ever said that. What they do say, and what we have to learn to say, is: "We're number one!" "We're number one!"

YOUNG MALE PROFESSIONAL CASH FLOW CHART

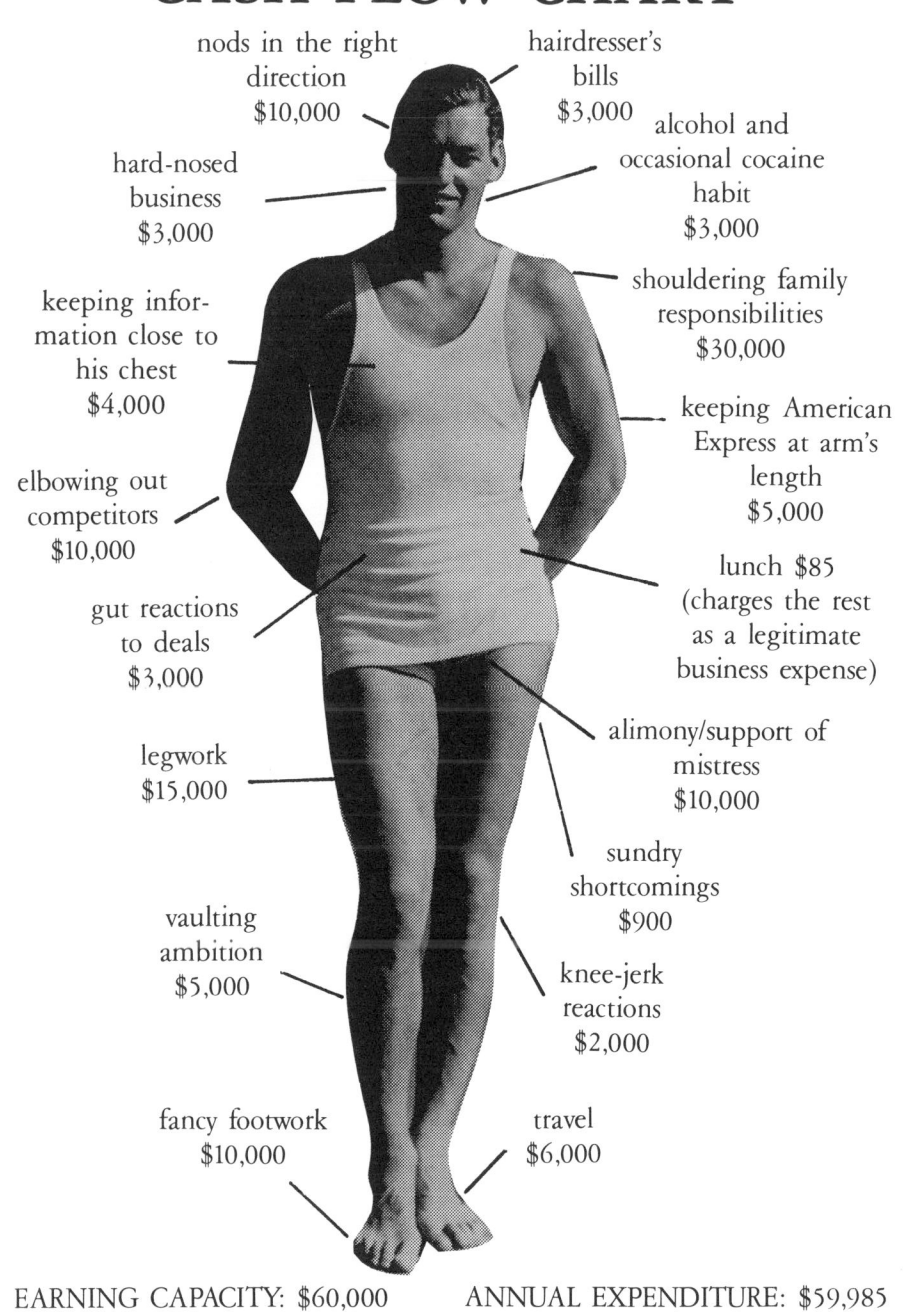

nods in the right
direction
$10,000

hairdresser's
bills
$3,000

alcohol and
occasional cocaine
habit
$3,000

hard-nosed
business
$3,000

keeping infor-
mation close to
his chest
$4,000

shouldering family
responsibilities
$30,000

keeping American
Express at arm's
length
$5,000

elbowing out
competitors
$10,000

lunch $85
(charges the rest
as a legitimate
business expense)

gut reactions
to deals
$3,000

legwork
$15,000

alimony/support of
mistress
$10,000

sundry
shortcomings
$900

vaulting
ambition
$5,000

knee-jerk
reactions
$2,000

fancy footwork
$10,000

travel
$6,000

EARNING CAPACITY: $60,000   ANNUAL EXPENDITURE: $59,985

NET PROFIT: $15

MEN
AT THE TOP

Behind every great man is a great woman, we are patronizingly told. So, it won't come as news to most women that it is the so-called weaker sex who constitute the coping stone of all successful endeavors, be they large or small. It is on our frail shoulders that men build their empires, using our intelligence, dedication, imagination, and loyalty as stepping-stones in their own successful careers.

The question we have to ask ourselves, if we are to rise to our natural place at the top, is not *why* men make use of our talents the way that they do (we all know the answer to that one) but *how* they do it. After all, if there's a method that works for the likes of them, it can only work better for us.

So how do they do it? The answer is surprisingly simple. All it takes is a well-cut suit and a remorseless stream of self-congratulatory small-talk that lasts anywhere from four or five years (if he's good) to thirty or so if, like most men, he is invincibly mediocre.

For women, small talk is almost always about other people; their health, their troubles and worries, their good news, and their bad. For men, it is always about themselves; their job, their prospects, their clients, their car, their connections, their hopes and desires. Occasionally it is about other men, especially those who are paid vast salaries for playing with bats, balls, and pucks. It is *never* about women (note: do not confuse men talking about sex with men talking about women).

All that we women have to do is jump onto this roller-coaster of self-promotion and out-boast the boasters. This shouldn't be hard. We're better than them at virtually everything else, everything else worthwhile that is; we'll let them keep on thrashing us at the shot-put, and they can continue with their monopoly in the military services. Hell, we'll even let them think they make the best chefs if it will make them feel more useful.

But where do we start on our voyage to the top? How do we begin to oust men from the comfortable positions that they have held for so long? It's easy. Just stick carefully to the following steps and in no time at all you will have your finger on the pulse of . . . well . . . whatever it is that you want your finger on the pulse of.

RULE ONE: TALK DIRTY

Talking dirty is merely the social bi-product of playing dirty. Men have known this for centuries. Whilst women have been expected to discreetly withdraw from dining rooms, locker rooms, and cabinet rooms, men have been getting down to the nitty-gritty behind our backs.

So don't let them get the upper hand. The minute they pretend to be discussing matters too heavy (and vulgar) for mere women's ears, immediately introduce into your conversation every four-letter word you can remember. Liberally sprinkle your discourse with anecdotes of such a rudimentary nature that even the most excretory of your male listeners will blush to hear them.

If you feel confident enough to provide crisp insights into the character and motives of male colleagues, go right ahead. If you can include smutty stories about their private lives (or even their private parts), all the better. Allude shamelessly to their comparative personal endowments; raise your eyebrows; give everyone a knowing wink. It will not be long before your victims are reduced to a mere male equivalent of that extra-mammary, typing-pool stereotype that men like to pretend exists.

RULE TWO: TALK BIG

The only way to command real authority is to talk big. Big talk is just the performance end of small talk. Chatter about performance contracts that have been decimated, deals that have been closed, profits that have

been made. And none of it could have happened without you. Let it be known that you have inside information about a Texaco share swindle. Smile condescendingly at those who have put their money in gilt-edged securities. And — why not? — do a little name-dropping. You are the woman who knows everyone. Male *poseurs* beware.

RULE THREE: BE AN EXPERT

OK, OK, so there's nothing more boring than "an expert." But you don't need to beat it to death. Just pick something arcane, and claim to be the "east coast consultant" or some such epithet. Use only jargon. Make sure that nobody understands a word that you say. They might suspect your conclusions, not to mention your motives, but they'll respect you for it. And in success circles, that's all that counts.

RULE FOUR: SCUTTLE COMPETITORS

Competition is what made this continent great, and no one knows this better than the men who've undermined their colleagues and associates as they strode past them to the top of the heap. Women have traditionally had poor stomachs for this kind of thing, but the time has come for us to take the bull by whatever part of his anatomy is convenient. The male business icon has to topple, and who is going to do it if not his female counterpart?

Let us live by what several American tabloids have known for years; that outrageous gossip and rumor are worth more than bland exposition and tedious debate any time.

So your first step is to slander your male competitor to such a degree that he not only secedes his job to you, but he will be forced to change his name, undergo plastic surgery and move to a Southern American country, using a forged Swiss passport.

Hint to management that you have heard rumors about your victim drinking whisky sours after midnight in gay bars. Say that witnesses have seen him dressed in women's underwear, dancing on tables. Or suggest that your immediate boss's eldest child looks more like your victim than his supposed father. Announce that your target holds among his acquaintances men who have been convicted for offenses against public decency. If you sling enough dirt, chances are that some of it will stick.

RULE FIVE: LEARN TO LIVE WITH YOURSELF

Mouthing off is how men have kept us oppressed for all these years, and it is a route that we have no choice but to follow if we want to become the masters of our masters. If you refuse to embrace this method, then you are even more lily-livered than I thought. It is time to stop being the nurturers. We must transcend our hormones and apply ourselves to establishing our proper place in the universe — at the top, where we belong.

Of course there are disadvantages. We will never be able to marry an intelligent and giving wife who will be prepared to take all the tedious, daily responsibilities off our shoulders, and greet us with smiles and a hot dinner when we get in from work. But then again, we will be rich enough and powerful enough to afford a cook and a psychiatrist.

And if we are ever tempted to feel bad about the new us, to yearn for the days when we were warm and giving, we must remind ourselves that — as men are so fond of telling us — "good guys finish last." Despite the adage, it is not cream that rises to the top; you only have to look at the nearest pond to see what really makes the grade.

GADGET JUNKIES

Born Under A Bad Appliance

Many men have a tendency to be gadget junkies, to be obsessed with mechanical or electronic gizmos that they consider toys. Men relate well to these gadgets; gadgets do not want anything from them, they do not wish to discuss relationships with them, and gadgets are submissive — they do whatever men want them to do without question. Men and machines are perfectly suited to each other. But how do *you* fit in? *The Definitive Guide to Men* is here to help you determine what type of man is attracted to a particular gadget. We rate the prospects of sharing a relationship with a man if he is obsessed with one of the following items.

THE TV REMOTE CONTROL UNIT
(The Box Commander)

The box commander will fight to the death for control of the remote unit as he feels naked and vulnerable without the box in his hand. He is an incessant channel flipper who randomly roams through the TV channels without purpose or design. He rarely consults the TV guide except for the sports schedule and heaven help you if you own a satellite dish!

Inevitably, while watching the movie you have been waiting for all week, and just as the *denouement* approaches, the box commander will flip to a border station to watch a Pepsi commercial in Spanish or see a slo-mo replay of a hockey fight. The commander type should be avoided at all costs.

THE POWERTOOL
(Mr. Fixit)

The problem with Mr. Fixit is that he insists on fixing it when it wasn't broken to begin with. He owns every tool known to man and eagerly awaits each new edition of the power tool catalogue. He considers his basement workshop the very center of his domestic life, his home and garden a construction site, and himself the architect and engineer. He is very handy when it comes to reinforcing bannisters, caulking windows, building birdfeeders, and turning wooden barrels into flowerpots. If, however, you actually need some real work done, best to call in a professional. Unless of course he has a large insurance policy and can be persuaded to rewire the main fuse box. This type is generally not recommended unless you happen to own several hundred shares of stock in Black and Decker.

THE COMPUTER
(Disk Brain)

Men who love to hack on their computers at home, are usually employed at a job where a knowledge of computers is essential. Therefore, we are dealing with someone who loves to do the same thing for twelve hours a day, seven days a week. Sound exciting?

He will usually look pale and unhealthy from staring at a computer screen all day, be flabby from his sedentary lifestyle, and will not relate well to other people due to his lack of social interaction. He calls his P.C. by the Christian name he has given "her" and likes her company better than anyone else's. He is reduced to a terrible sulk when deprived of her presence during power failures. But, hey, if "closing a file" is your idea of foreplay, this disk brain is for you.

THE VCR
(Captain Video)

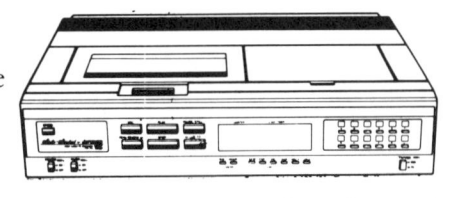

Did you miss the TV pilot of "My Two Dads, " or an episode of "Star Trek: The New Generation?" Well, don't worry, this guy has it all on video. Anything you can possibly think of (but never want to see), he's got it and he flaunts it: his Aunt Bertha and Uncle Ernie's 40th wedding anniversary; his nephew's bar mitzvah; every episode of "The Twilight Zone" and a project he personally produced: a special two-hour tribute to Andy Rooney. His wildest dream in life is to have one of his film shorts shown on Dick and Ed's "Bloopers and Practical Jokes."

A relationship with this man and his camera and VCR is not recommended, unless of course, you want full documentary coverage of every second of your life, your children's lives, your orthodontist's life . . . .

THE SOUND SYSTEM
(Mr. Component)

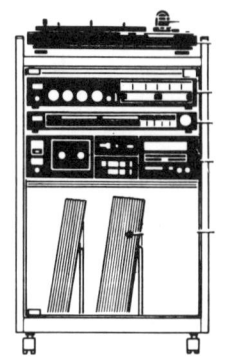

This man's main ambition in life is high-fidelity sound. He keeps abreast of the latest developments in state of the art stereo components, spends countless hours in audio shops discussing the merits of one system over another, and is constantly upgrading his personal system at great expense. His home is built around his stereo, which is always on. So, if you happen to share the same taste in music, this type is, at worst, a bore. He is, by far, preferable to the box commander and not that bad a choice for a mate.

THE GARDEN TOOL
(John Lawnboy)

For every garden tool, there is a season, and a purpose, and John Lawnboy has them all, and uses them in his quest for the perfect landscape surrounding his home; his castle. In the spring, a time to rake and sow; in the summer, to weed, cut and water; in the fall, to harvest and rake; and,

in the winter, time to rev up the snow blower. This type is highly recommended, because while he improves your property value he's out of the house and therefore out of your hair.

CAR GIZMOS
(Tony Camaro)

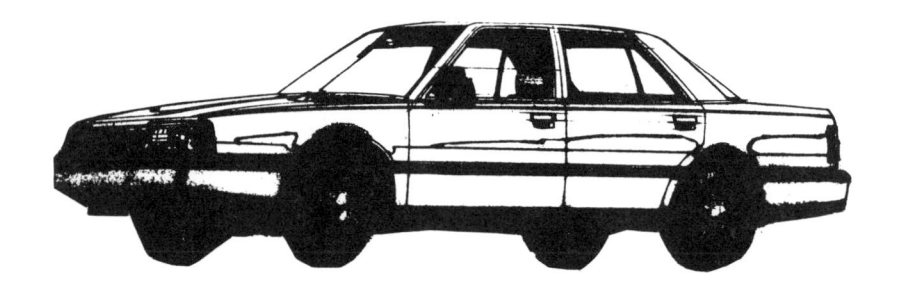

Life began for Tony the first time he touched a stick shift, turned on the ignition, and felt the dumb, powerful beast beneath him throb into life. He can effortlessly disassemble and reassemble a V8 or V6 engine, and he spends almost all of his spare time in his garage working on his car, or at the local car dealer's parts department. He is absolutely neurotic about any "ping," "clunk," or "hiss" that emanates from under the hood of his car. He is far too emotionally involved with his carburetor for you to consider a realistic prospect for a fulfilling relationship. Not recommended.

THE CAR-MASUTRA MALE DRIVING POSITIONS

One of the most damaging aspects of the hurly-burly of modern Western living is the often long and tiresome rush-hour drives to and from work. The following recently-discovered exercise routine for male drivers is a totally new concept in which male folk wisdom meets Eastern therapeutic medicine.

These positions can be practised using only a high-backed kitchen chair. When you feel comfortable with them, you may try them in a stationary vehicle. When you have perfected this ancient craft, then you should be able to adopt these positions at will any time while you are driving. You'll discover that soon you will start to feel egotistical and assertive, and you will arrive at your destination feeling fulfilled and superior.

1. Right hand on the wheel, left hand in the crotch

2. Right hand on the wheel, left elbow on the window sill

3. Right hand on the wheel, left arm out of the window,
hand resting on roof

4. Left hand on the wheel, right arm across the passenger seat
(nicknamed The Salesman Position)

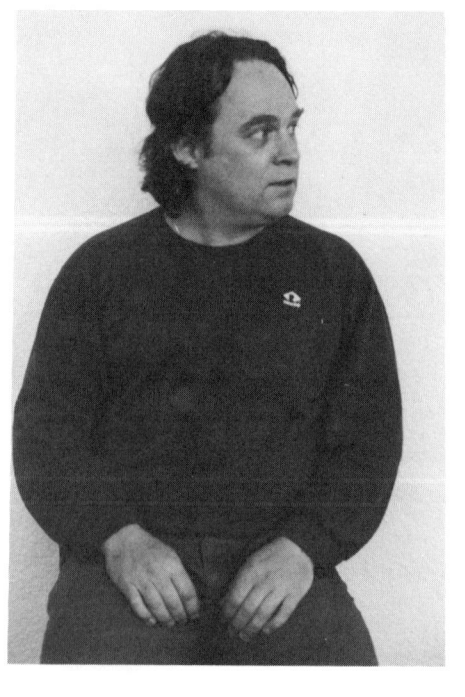

5. The special traffic light position.
Foot on brake,
both hands in the crotch,
edging forward slightly
by releasing the brake
intermittently

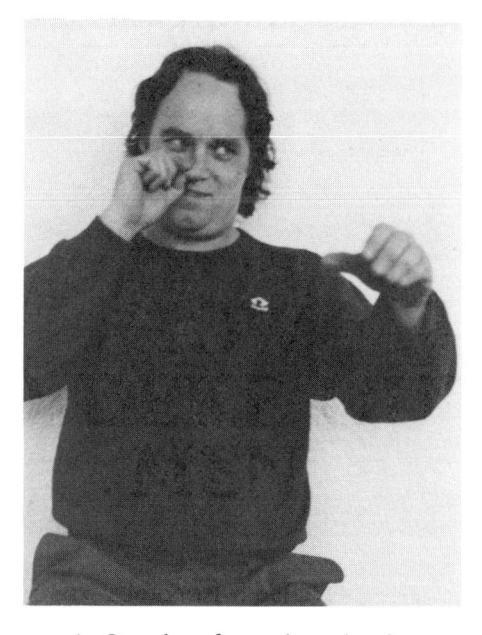

6. One hand on the wheel,
index finger of the free hand firmly inserted in the nose

7. One hand on the wheel,
with the free hand holding a bottle of beer to the lips
(advanced students may try this with a martini)

MALE STEREOTYPES
RICH MAN, POOR MAN, PLAYBOY, GEEK

THE JOCK

The jock plays, watches, and lives for sports. He subscribes to *Sports Illustrated, Golf* magazine, and *Hustler.* He understands the *need* for violence in professional sports, owns a large screen TV, and reads the sports section of the newspaper first. He can quote obscure baseball, football, or hockey stats effortlessly, yet is unable to complete his own income tax form. When he is not watching a game on TV, he is playing on some amateur sports team which he believes will vault him into the big leagues. His life ambitions include a low cholesterol level, a full head of hair, and appearing in a beer commercial. His idea of foreplay is turning off the TV.

THE ALAN ALDA TYPE

Has little or no chest hair and has had a vasectomy by the time he reaches his 33rd birthday. He shares the domestic chores and child rearing tasks equally with his wife — but only in public. He subscribes to *Ms Magazine,* HBO, and *Bleeding Heart Weekly.* The charities he supports include Save the Whales, Greenpeace, and the Hollywood Squares Pension Fund. He is a member of National Organization for Women, the ACLU, and the American Automobile Association. Oh, and the wife works!

THE PROFESSOR

He is usually Caucasian and middle-class. He doesn't own a TV, corning ware, or soap-on-a-rope. He can be all things to all people — especially to attractive, young, nubile, undergraduate females. He is a nihilist who doesn't believe in anything but himself. He is the only type of man who can read silently without moving his lips.

THE PLAYBOY

He is the sum total of the size of his penis. The Playboy's sexual ego is only exceeded by the weight of his jewelry. He drives a sports car — usually a Corvette or a Porsche; frequents singles bars, supermarkets, and abortion clinics. He spends most of his money on his car, his clothes, his jewelry, and his tanning salon. He has a *National Enquirer* IQ and believes that he is so virile that he can impregnate a woman by merely glancing at her from across the room. His only concession to women's rights is to always carry a condom in his wallet.

THE EXECUTIVE TYPE

Cannot conceive of a sentence without himself as the subject and money as the object. He defines himself in terms of his net worth and his position in the company. By his late twenties he can no longer remove the brown stains from the tip of his nose. He talks endlessly about nothing, using whatever lingo is peculiar to his industry. He never reveals anything personal about himself and considers being called a "workaholic," "a corporate henchman," or "ruthless," a compliment. He subscribes to *Fortune, The Wall Street Journal, The Squash Review,* and *Soldier of Fortune,* but all his magazines are delivered to the office. The only evidence of his existence at home is the dirty ring around his shirt collars in the "little woman's" laundry basket.

THE GODFATHER

He is as romantic as the Ayatollah Khomeini and as personable as Ed Sullivan. His word is law and his will will be done and heaven help the woman married to this type of man. His idea of foreplay is to demand sex. His ideal woman is twenty-one, pregnant, and has huge hunga-dungas. He

subscribes to Penthouse, Playboy, and *Law and Order Weekly.* His favorite TV show is "The Price is Right," he is a member of the National Rifle Association and lobbies against the ERA. His heroes are John Wayne, Oliver North Sylvester Stallone, and Genghis Khan.

"Considering he's the Gay Right's first contestant, it's not a bad effort."

SELF-IMAGE: A MAN'S MOST IMPORTANT ASSET

There's nothing either good or bad, but thinking makes it so.
William Shakespeare

Isn't it just like a man to think that all he has to do is to think that something is the way that he wants it to be in order to make it a reality.

With men, it's all image; and assuming a role that fits in with their self-image is a man's strength, not his weakness. It is in their conformity with perfect self-images that their belief in male superiority lies.

Mind you, TV shows have done nothing to help. Have you noticed how men are portrayed in all the modern family sitcoms? Take a look at "Cosby," "Family Ties," "Growing Pains," or "Roseanne," and what do you get? Bossy, irascible mothers and nurturing, sensitive, hen-pecked husbands and fathers. Worse still, men are starting to believe this propaganda. They are adjusting their self-image to include the perfect, understanding parent among their many talents. The housewife and mother role — men's one concession to women's superiority — they have also now taken for themselves.

But we are not afraid. We know that "thinking has made it so." We also know that their hold on all their other roles is just as tenuous. We can see through them all.

THE PROFESSIONAL

Any man who goes to work in a suit and tie will always be too busy to take on any responsibilities in the home. He is a business professional, and business professionals are permanently swamped with work.

Try this experiment: call him from any part of the house, and he will reply "hold on a minute, I'm busy." Doing what? Cleaning out the toilet? Stripping the bed? When challenged, he will tell you that he's "checking out some figures," which probably means that he was reading *Playboy*.

THE GREAT INTELLECT

This wit and *raconteur* is unable to participate in the superficial business of everyday life because he is deep in thought. He is rarely seen without a book; this is especially true when he is heading to the bathroom. He has nothing but contempt for his colleagues who are merely stuffy academics with delusions of *grandeur*. He would die a thousand deaths if you ever showed him the photograph that you are hoarding for the right moment which shows him with his finger up his nose at a neighbor's barbecue.

THE PUNK

At first glance this fellow is an enigma. How are we to understand a man who slips into a pair of black spandex tights, drapes toilet chains around his waist, and then looks into his mirror and declares "yes, that's it — the very effect I was aiming at."

But do not be deceived by this competitive man who wears more eye make-up and jewelry than you do. This fellow sees himself as the Picasso of the fashion world;

he is on the lookout for your reaction. So do not lean forward in order to catch the drift of his mumblings. Not only do you run the risk of losing an eye to his spiked hair, he is only going to ask you what kind of woman dates a man who wears office supplies.

ONE OF THE BOYS

Here we have the life and soul of the party. When he pictures himself, it is in a vibrant setting surrounded by hoards of people, who think he's real fun to be with. In secret, he lives in fear of being thought a stuffed shirt. He will go to any lengths to assure himself of his popularity. He will spend your grocery money buying rounds of drinks, and will be the first one to drop his pants and dance on the bar in his underwear if one of the guys were to suggest that this might be amusing.

FOREIGNERS

A word is necessary here about men who claim to be foreigners. Be extra wary of them. Most male foreigners are not foreigners at all, but merely *poseurs* who feel exotic. It is true that many men do have foreign blood if you go back enough generations, but you will soon discover that they pose as foreigners only to make themselves appear more interesting. That they believe their own advertising is their problem. Make sure that they do not make it yours.

For example, a man whose great-grandfather was born in East Germany will most likely prefix his name with "doctor" when he first meets you. This will tell you that he wants you to fear and respect him. Other Eastern European men like to call themselves "Count" or "Baron," although this harmless little habit is easy to check out, and a rather obvious delusion.

Men whose families hark back to western Europe are more interested in impressing you with their family tree. When they look in the mirror, they see centuries of regal bearing reflected proudly back. The adoption of the French "de," German "von," and Dutch "van," are well-known crowd-pleasers, but you shouldn't let them get to you. They all mean "of," and tell you merely where your *poseur* comes from. So big deal. We all come from somewhere.

British men enjoy the habit of hyphenating their surnames "Smythe-Jones," or adding MBE, DFC, or KGB (in the case of the less practised ones and the ones who have attended Cambridge university). This is supposed to give the impression of social standing and success. The fact is that virtually all English people can trace their roots back to some Earl or Viscount; the nobility have a long and historic tradition of producing children out of wedlock. Tell this to Smythe-Jones, OBE, and his ego will deflate audibly.

Italian men need special attention because they are unusually dangerous. They have read somewhere that "Italians are the world's greatest lovers," and they spend a considerable number of their man (and woman) hours trying to live up to this impossible adage. They are easy to confront, however. If you suspect that this man is spinning you a line, tell him that you are going to check with his mother. He will break down and confess immediately that he runs a dry goods store, that he rides there on a motorscooter every morning, and that he's only ever slept with women in his dreams.

MR. COULD HAVE BEEN

Who among us hasn't heard this one? "I could have been playing in the majors now if I hadn't broken my ankle the day before the Astros' talent scout came to watch my team." He is cousin to the man who claims to have been brilliant in high school science, only to have been deprived of an astonishing and successful career by being forced, instead, to work in a cookie factory to support his aging parents. Ah, what these men could have been, given the opportunities that others had . . . . And, as they fall asleep at night, they do so to the roar of a crowd chanting their name. He has pitched yet another perfect game. He has taken home his third Nobel prize. Effortlessly. Justly. The real him.

SO WHAT?

So what does it tell us, this male preoccupation with image? Nothing that we didn't all know before. Only that men live at the center of their own inflated, imaginary universes, and that they expect to live at the center of ours. And, that ringing down the halls of history, from John Donne to Ernest Hemingway, to the man in your life, men have not sent to ask for whom the bell tolls, because they know that — like everything else — it tolls for them.

THE
HISTORY
HALL OF SHAME

We may as well admit it now. The history of the world is the history of men; from the beginning of time, men have had it all. And we women are left wondering, after all of the opportunities that men have had to change the world for the better, why they persist in making such a dog's dinner of it.

Let's look at it another way. Whenever our mate, or spouse, or boyfriend irritates us we occasionally hear ourselves admonishing them with "Oh, you men — you're all the same!" Of course, even as we say it, we know it isn't true. What we really mean to say is "you're all as bad," which is a different story altogether.

It was the indisputably male Carl Jung, after all, who claimed that man had a common consciousness, and we only have to look at what he has done throughout history to understand just how common it's been.

Nevertheless, men pride themselves on the fact that even if their decisions have been historically questionable, they have always been momentous. But this is not so. Men leave behind them a trail of petty actions, the memory of which no amount of time can erase. What follows is only a partial list of things that men have done that wins them a permanent place in the History Hall of Shame.

1225 B.C.

Ramses II of Egypt gives the official go-ahead to history's first brewer. Within two years, beer is the Egyptian national beverage.

530 B.C.

Pythagoras leaves to posterity the notion that the square on the hypotenuse of a right-angled triangle is equal to the sum of the squares on the other two sides. Since this date it has been the habit of all mankind to look back on their schooldays and wonder why it is we all need to know this.

51 B.C.

Julius Caesar writes a book about the Gallic Wars, and starts the trend of celebrity publishing.

727 A.D.

The Duke Orso becomes the first ruler of Venice. From now on, men begin to think that taking them for boat rides will induce in women a romantic willingness to be compromised.

1066

Harold II is killed at the Battle of Hastings by an arrow through the eye. This frankly showy way of meeting his death has provided unwitting students with the first historical date considered necessary to memorize subsequent to the birth of Christ.

1493

Columbus colonizes South America, initiating almost five hundred years of oppression. As a result Hispanic literature becomes required reading in some North American university programs.

1812

Napoleon Bonaparte invades Russia, giving rise to the now-accepted idea that it is OK for short men to compensate for their height with globally-aggressive behavior.

1819

Romantic poet John Keats diagnosed as consumptive. Until this date, tuberculosis had been considered an exclusively female disorder because of it's required displays of sensitivity, languishing, and fatalism. These traits now become available to men.

1875

Austrian health freak, Friedrich Haberlandt, introduces the soybean to Europe, starting a health-food trend than the world never recovers from.

1922

Rudolph Valentino appears in the silent movie *The Young Rajah*; women realize that men are even more attractive if they wear few clothes and keep their mouths shut. Unhappily, this discovery is supressed, and is quickly followed by the hurried invention of the "talkies."

1943

Oppenheimer leaves a note for his wife in their Los Alamos condo: "Gone fission."

1959

Richie Valens dies only *after* giving the world "La Bamba." Great timing, Richie.

1989

Libya's General Khadafi proves — one more time — that you don't have to be smart, good-looking, or even sane to wage wars. You just have to be a man.

An historic moment
"One small step for Elvis Presley . . . ."

WHY DO MEN THINK WE LIKE IT WHEN

They patronize us about how far women have come in recent years.

They offer to *help* us with the dishes. What makes them think that dirty dishes are ours?

They creep up behind us and fondle us when we're doing household chores.

They offer us flowers after an argument instead of an apology.

They tell us that we're at our sexiest when we're eight-and-a-half months pregnant.

THE PENILE COLONY
Men's Top Ten Favorite Names for their Penises

10. dick
9. prick
8. knob
7. weinie
6. boner

5. the family jewels
4. main muscle
3. cock
2. crowd pleaser
1. Mr. Happy

ALSO RANS

magic wand, salami, schlong, dong, whopper, rocketship, shaft, pecker, blow torch, and the Washington Monument

MALE JEOPARDY

How often have you found yourself in the following situation:

You and two of your female friends or associates from work are sitting in a bar, at a corner table, having a quiet drink. The three of you have been talking and laughing for an hour or so, completely absorbed in the conversation at your table and oblivious to what is happening around you.

Without warning, or provocation, a man appears at your table. He asks a question to which you respond with one of the following sentences.

— Piss off, dick-brain.
— Why do men always assume that women are more interested in male companionship than female companionship?
— Wow! We're really glad you dropped by our table. You're just in time for refills.
— You know, your type of person is the reason why the pill was invented in the first place.
— Not now. Perhaps you should come back after you've completed those penis enhancing exercises the doctor ordered.
— Yes, we'd love some company, but do you really think that you can handle three at the same time.

Now, Question Number One is: What was his question?
And Question Number Two is: What did he expect?

Answers:
1. Would you ladies like some company for this evening?
2. Adoration, praise, and fellatio.

BETE-A-TETE

Gender stereotyping begins at birth and continues throughout life. The worst insult flung at a little boy is the accusation that he is acting like "a little girl." This disapproval of feminine traits by little boys is so commonplace that it is widely accepted as normal.

Girls are "crybabies," "sissies," "weak," "boring," and "stupid." Little boys are encouraged to "be strong," "take risks," "be aggressive," and "to explore."

Sociologists, psychiatrists and the like would have us believe that this is because children respond to the expectations of adults in a misogynistic world. Maybe so, but this explanation fails to take into account that every male is born with two personalities: Dr. Jekyll and Mr. Penis. And depending upon the predominance of one character over the other, a man is either ruled by his intellect, at which time he is capable of receiving some signals from outside his gender (but only on a very rudimentary level), or by his genitalia, a condition commonly known as being a "dick-brain."

Unfortunately, about 99% of men are dick-brains, but if you are unsure how to classify a particular male, just find out if he refers to his penis in the third person. If he does, than he is most definitely a dick-brain.

At the very core of a dick-brain's existence lies his sexual organ, sometimes flaccid, lying limply to the right or the left depending upon which

side he dresses, or standing erect, like a flagpole that his enslaved psyche proudly salutes. Men regard their penises with nationalistic fervor as they would a country, or a political belief. Although a man's testicles are his own and his most vulnerable part, the penis is somehow distinct. It has a life and a personality all of its own. It is a divining rod that steers the attached individual. It is a lone-star general going forth into battle while the obedient doughboy — or what's left of him anyway — follows meekly behind.

Although men would have us believe that they are the ventriloquist and Mr. Penis the wooden dummy, we know that the opposite is true. Men are slaves to the only visible attribute they are born with. Behind every great penis is a vulnerable man that will do anything to ensure that his diabolical twin survives and flourishes. In fact, it could be said that the male intellect (such as it is) is merely Mr. Penis's bodyguard and publicist.

Now given this, how is enlightened communication between the sexes possible? After all, it is this separate entity, General Penis, that encounters the only intimate contact that most males ever experience with women — sexual intercourse. For an update on the consequences of this, see *The Definitive Guide to Men*'s "Sex in the 1990s."

NOT
THE MARRYING
KIND

If there's one tedious line that most of we women are sick to death of hearing, it's the pathetic male assertion that they're "not the marrying kind." As we all know, nothing is further from the truth. All men are the marrying kind. They would have to be insane not to be. Would you turn down the opportunity to have a live-in, unpaid domestic servant with wage-earning and child-bearing capabilities? Of course you wouldn't. Nor would they; they just don't want to admit it.

But rather than confess that they are relieved to have found a woman who will take care of "the little things" in their lives — cleaning the toilet, remembering their father's birthday, picking their underwear off the bedroom floor — virtually all men prefer to make women feel guilty (for having tied them down) and grateful that they have chosen us to share their little things with (usually, their little things are hardly worth the effort — see SEDUCTION).

In fact, it is we women who should profess to not being the marrying kind. We have so little to gain. We can keep house, hold down a full-time job, bear children, and remember our parents' birthdays without the benefit of testosterone. And don't let *him* persuade you otherwise. Take a stand. Inform him that relationships progress through four stages, and that none of them requires marriage. Then proceed to live by the following principles.

1. SEDUCTION: TYING THE KNOT

It is not true that men seldom make passes at girls who wear glasses; men make passes at anything that is not considered medically dead. So the first step is to make sure that *you* are the one doing the seducing, not him. This does not mean that you are forced henceforth to date only weenies. Far from it. Obsequiousness is only desirable in a man if he is a waiter or a shoe-salesman (unfortunately, very few of *them* demonstrate this highly desirable trait). Servility in a man is most pleasurable when he is not fully aware of what he has been reduced to. It is the gift that keeps on giving.

A word of warning, however; when choosing a seducee, don't be swayed by his anatomical attributes. I know it's tempting, but it's a joy that soon passes. And I hardly need remind most of you that sex is rarely as good as it sounds, and never as good as you imagined.

So avoid Mediterranean playboys at all costs. Although they are often unashamedly lecherous, those smoldering looks will do you no good. If you allow yourself to become a victim of this kind of man's *double entendres* and other various come-on lines, you are a lost cause, and I am wasting my breath.

Now, as most women know, there are two kinds of seduction; seduction for pleasure and seduction for fiscal advancement. When choosing the one that is right for you, let your moral predilections and the current state of your bank account be your guide. As for technique — you don't need me to tell you what to do; we all know our individual strengths.

For those women who wish to compromise their seducee with a view to palimony, it is first necessary to choose a target-rich environment; the racket club, or the beach at Malibu if you can afford it. Remember, the

more carefully you choose, the less frequently you are going to have to go through this.

2. EXPLOITATION: LIVING WITH THE KNOT

The first rule of exploitation is *never do anything for a man out of the goodness of your heart.* He will only take advantage of it. He will tell you that you have never had it so good, in the hope that it will take your mind off the fact that you've never had it at all. So don't play his game; make him play yours.

This means that there is no reason for you ever to do his laundry. Never cook. Nor — in turn — should you let him try to kid you that he's a *gourmet* chef; this is only his way of getting out of spending good money on you in the kind of restaurant in which you deserve to be seen.

For clues, look around his kitchen and you'll be able to see at a glance that his minimal cooking facilities, multiplied by what you have already recognized as his nonexistent culinary imagination would soon lead to a long-term menu of such super-human constancy that it would send Julia Child screaming for refried beans. And, if it's not good enough for Julia, it certainly isn't good enough for you.

Of course, sex becomes a problem at this stage of a relationship. Now that your quarry has been successfully seduced, sex has fulfilled its purpose, and, as a result, it loses its attraction. Your eyes begin to wander to other prey. This cannot be helped.

Adultery is probably the best way of coping with this kind of stress. After all, we women already have enough pressures to cope with, without adding to them.

Don't give in to guilt. And don't fall for his nauseating stream of romantic flattery. We've heard it all before. Tell him to put his money where his mouth is. After all, men never tire of telling us that they are thinkers and philosophers. So recognize in your man his existential desire to be burdened.

Lead him to his fate. It will only do him good.

3. EXTRICATION: UNTYING THE KNOT

Getting out of an unwanted relationship is often considered the most difficult of its four stages, but for the skilled operative it can be the most fun as well as the most rewarding.

For married people, this has always been the most inconvenient stage of their relationship. Unfortunately for us, our western society has been painfully dilatory about adopting a wise and useful habit that has long since been acceptable in Arabian circles. In this sage and ancient culture, it is enough for a disappointed spouse to repeat three times to their no-longer-loved-one "I divorce thee," and before you can say "my husband's a real Shiite," you're home free with a villa in Mecca and sacks of gold trinkets for consolation prizes.

This time-saving method of separation saves a fortune in lawyer's fees, not to mention countless hours being consoled in darkened bars by men you'll blanche to remember twenty-four hours later.

Since our society has not yet adopted this civilized approach to divorce, our best option is to stay single. For those wise women who have successfully completed stages one and two of their relationship without having to resort to marriage, this next, more liberating stage will make you look and feel years younger.

The first hint that you have reached the extrication stage of your relationship is when *he* asks you if you'd mind staying in this Saturday night while he watches the World Series on TV. Your eyes will glaze over. You will already sense the musty after-smell of beer and sweat. Soon he will suggest that you share a bag of plain potato chips.

If you let it get this far, he will next try to convince you that his bisexuality and cocaine addiction will not get in the way of a happy and fulfilling relationship. After that . . . God knows what might happen. I leave it to your imagination.

By the time your relationship has reached this point, suffice it to say that there is no more time to argue; the moment to assert yourself is past. All you can do is cut your losses at supersonic speed. Don't linger over the goodbye. Don't wait for an invitation to listen to "As Time Goes By" at an airport in the mist. If you hesitate too long, next Saturday you will be dining at a local pizza parlor or — worse —at the sign of the golden arches.

Most men take rejection rather badly. If you are the kind who insists on feeling sorry for him, pass him on to a girlfriend who's not as smart as you. Or write his phone number in the women's toilets at your local bar. In time he'll thank you for it.

If he starts to cry, it's time for Draconian measures. Unfortunately, this is the stage at which some women resort to violence. However, I recommend that you merely run for your life. If you're going to have to spend money hiring a lawyer, it's preferable to require one for fiscal litigation than for defense against a murder charge.

And, last of all, *never* be afraid that if you leave him you'll end up alone. It's when you're *with* him that you're really alone. Think about it.

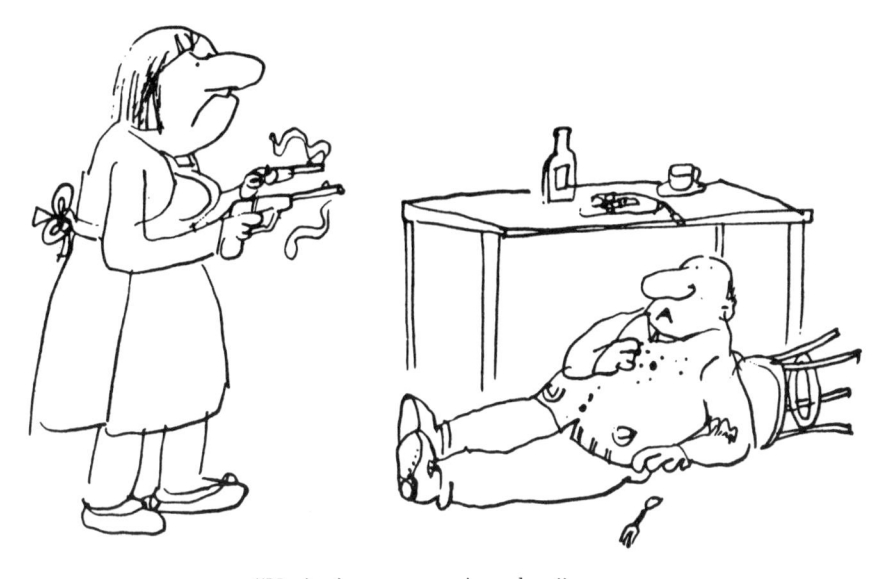

"You're just overreacting, dear."

4. CELEBRATION: LOOKING FOR NEW KNOTS

Now comes the fun part; starting over. Your personal life is going to be a romantic smorgasbord; a financial and emotional buffet.

Those of you who have completed this course of action for profit should abandon your present location and move on. It is best to leave hunting grounds to lie fallow for a year or two before attempting a second plunder.

For those women who are simple pleasure-seekers, do be careful not to get the reputation for being a woman who is rather too easily accessible. When men offer you money, they should not be expecting it to be on a fee for service basis.

So off you go; you are now prepared for a bright and successful future. And remember, if there are ten wealthy and available people in a room, nine of them will be men. And eight of *them* will be suckers.

7 QUESTIONS ABOUT MEN THAT WOMEN CAN'T ANSWER

Why do men think you believe them when they say they buy *Penthouse* and *Playboy* for the articles and interviews?

Why, in espionage books and movies, do cynical, middle-aged, overweight male spies always manage to attract 20-year-old, gorgeous, intelligent blonde women?

Why do men never know when their household has run out of milk, or bread, or anything else?

Why do men's feet smell so bad?

Why do men need forty-five minutes to have a bowel movement?

Why do men always fall asleep immediately after sex?

Why are men so afraid of seeming vulnerable?

WHEN HE SAYS — HE REALLY MEANS

WHEN HE SAYS	HE REALLY MEANS
What are *we* having for supper?	What are *you* making for supper?
Are we out of ketchup?	Will you go and look for it?
I might go to the game on Friday.	I've already bought the tickets and I'm meeting my pals at the stadium at 7:30.
My wife doesn't understand me.	I wish my wife didn't understand me so well.
I'm interested in you.	I'm interested in your body.
I don't know why this has happened. It's never happened before.	This is the first time I've been to bed with a woman who makes more money that I do.

SEX
IN THE
1990s

Sexual behavior has changed drastically since the 1960s. In those days neither parents nor educators saw any great need to enlighten pubescent youngsters about matters of the heart or other organs located slightly to the north or south.

But even in those days, boys had access to a fairly large range of sources of information about sex and women's bodies: their fathers (who had reached puberty in the mid-fifties and loved to tell their sons about their time "behind the stadium with the high school slut"), *Playboy* magazine, the local garage mechanic's wall calendar — or for the especially desperate, *National Geographic* could always be consulted in a pinch.

But girls were not so lucky. Mothers were not very forthcoming about sex as something other than a way to produce offspring (the topic was received with the same sort of enthusiasm as bed-wetting or a confession to belonging to the Communist Party). *Playgirl* magazine had yet to be invented and women's magazines were still pushing "40 New Ways to Serve Leftovers" as a reason to subscribe.

Although there were a few among that generation of females who pretended to know what "69" really meant, all they were really cognizant of was its numerical value. They knew what sexual intercourse was, they'd had a very clinical description of it provided by Miss Ima Prude in Grade 9 hygiene class. But what all those sexual terms that sounded so exotic really

meant were well beyond their realm of knowledge. In fact very few of the sexual side dishes that the 60s popularized were known by young women until they were actually experiencing them.

The pill emancipated women from the fear of pregnancy and gave women the opportunity to explore their sexuality. The female half of the love generation threw itself into the sexual revolution with complete abandon and great enthusiasm.

Men were taken by surprize when women began demanding sexual satisfaction and more foreplay, or at least something more than what passes as mating in an episode of "Wild Kingdom." Suddenly men became accountable, they were held responsible to provide the wherewithall for women to achieve orgasm.

Indeed, three important things happened during that period: 1. women began to talk about sex; 2. women began to have lots of sex; 3. women began to talk to other women about the performances of the men they were having sex with.

Men were not prepared for the sexual demands made by women. They did not know how to respond to their openness and honesty. Men had never had to account to anyone, let alone their previously submissive partners, for their sexual performances. Men had kept sex simple and uncomplicated for centuries.

He called the shots, she submitted to his will. Get it in, get it on, take it out. It was goal-oriented, like hitting a home run, or passing a drivers' test. Men had never learned to enjoy the process of courtship, only the outcome.

Women's demands were making sex too complex and confusing. Furthermore, men misinterpreted women's demands as an attempt to "take over" the dominant role — to be the boss in the relationship. Men responded with hostility when all women really wanted was equal pay-off for equal work. (Mind you men have yet to wrap their minds around that concept.)

Men felt threatened and vulnerable, the rules of sexual conduct were changing and they weren't the ones dictating the rules. It was all the more upsetting for men because they still truly believed in all the sexual myths about women that they had perpetuated over the years, namely:
— the mere sight of their magnificent members is enough to reduce a woman

to putty in their masculine hands
— women can be depended upon to lie passively on their backs while men do the humping
— women are not capable of enjoying sex
— a woman must be sedated or drunk before she will submit to sex
— if she willingly submits to sex she's a whore

Thus it came as a complete surprize to men when women began to assert their sexuality openly and loudly. After centuries of silence and obedience, women were ordering men to wake up and smell the coitus — and the odor left a lot to be desired.

During the next two decades academics and sexologists published numerous studies about male and female sexuality — their desires, wishes, dreams, and fears were well-documented for the opposite sex to see. Some men did attempt to be better lovers — they learned the latest dance steps and began to blow-dry their hair. However, their sexual behavior continued to be more suitable for bears in the woods than a woman's boudoir.

Tenderness and sensitivity continued to remain low in the list of qualities that men aspired to. The only significant change that occurred during this time was one of nuance. Previously a woman gone "bad" was a woman who did "it" a lot, with many different partners. A slut, in fact. At some point, the definition changed. A "bad" woman was now someone who demanded sexual satisfaction from her partner, and if she didn't get it, she'd tell him and everyone else about it.

By the mid-1980s, horrific sexually transmitted diseases and the AIDS virus arrived just in time to save men from having to come to terms with women's sexuality. And as we head into the 1990s fear of these dread diseases demands that partners practise "safe sex."

"Safe sex" is monogamous sex, married sex. We are heading back to an era when sex before marriage is taboo — straight back to the 1950s, only both parties will be slightly more knowledgeable about sex in theory — as both will probably be virgins on their wedding night. But if that is the price men have to pay to keep women in line, they seem quite willing to pay it. Safe sex is only really safe when undertaken by virginal and inexperienced partners who, of course, have no basis for comparison.

But that's all right, although she might be disappointed in the bedroom, she fell in love with his laugh, his eyes, his eager mind — he fell in love with her huge tits and tight ass.

"Oh no! Not *that* old cliché again."

TAPPING
THE
MOTHER LOAD

If there's one thing that every woman knows it's that for every man who yearns to be married, there's a mother who can't stand the idea. Yet — have you noticed — just about all mother-in-law jokes are about *women's* mothers? Men do not abuse their mothers in public because their relationship with her is sacred. She is his protector, and he is her little boy. And you are the siren come to lure him away. No matter what she says, she will never forgive you for it. So, ignore her gushing welcomes, her expensive gifts, her boasts about you to relatives and neighbors; it's all a front. This woman hates you more than she can say. She is your enemy.

But don't despair. You can win if you approach this problem properly. Rather than trying to win her over to your side, the key to coping with this paragon of oedipal power is to cut her off at the pass. Once you've managed to figure out where she's coming from, you have a better chance of making her stay there.

MEN WILL BE BOYS

OK, OK, so there's nothing more revolting than hearing your unshaven, beer-bellied mate being called "my baby boy" by a mother who refuses to acknowledge that he's grown up. But it's not as simple as it seems. What she's really doing is letting you know that she understands him better than you do; that there was a time when he needed her more than he

needs you. So, when she takes you on one of her interminable trips down memory lane which feature her baby boy stumbling, drooling and inarticulate, across the dining room floor, interject with "I know, I know. He's like that when he comes home after 'Monday Night Football' with his pals. Isn't it *cute*." His past will soon become a closed book.

Under no circumstances must you ever criticize baby boy's behavior in front of his mother. You'll have plenty of time for that when you get him home. After all, you have to keep him on your side. Don't forget, it is she who has made him what he is today. In that weakness lies your strength.

MAKING THE GRADE

If you show no signs of giving her boy up, the more astute mother will regale you with a litany of his faults and defects that, she's sure, are going to drive you crazy. She will complain about him incessantly. She will tell you that he has accomplished nothing in life and that you're not to expect anything from a life with him except unhappiness and hardship. She will not say so, but she numbers you among the bad choices he has made. She says she can't imagine why you stay with him. And she's desperately hoping that you won't.

If she can't get through to you, she will extend her audience to friends and relatives. She will complain to them when you are unable to correct in him those irritating habits that she developed when he was young. When he doesn't phone her for weeks on end, she will blame you for not reminding him. She is hoping to nag you into forcing him to pay more attention to his filial duties. Don't fall into this trap. Leave him alone. Just gloat and enjoy your victory.

CHANGING THE RULES

When she can't get you to feel bad about *him*, she'll try to make you feel bad about yourself. She will greet you with, "My goodness, have you put on weight?" or "What *have* you done to your hair?" She won't wait for an answer. Instead, she will launch into a history of her aches and pains; she will tell you in detail about personal problems that you'd prefer not to hear. So don't let it get this far. As soon as you walk into the same room as her, start to talk about yourself. Tell her how amazed your colleagues are

that your relationship with her son is so successful, especially since you are a highly-respected brain surgeon and he is merely a window-cleaner. Laugh about his vulgar little foibles (choose one that he shares with the rest of his family), and finish by offering to tell her the brand name of a new facial depilatory that you've seen advertised for older women. From this point on, she will avoid you like the plague.

"You've gone too far this time, David. Here comes his mother."

SEX

This is where you're always going to win hands down. His relationship with his mother is the only aspect of a man's life that is not dominated by sex. In fact, the subject is virtually taboo. Almost all mothers are convinced that their boy isn't having sex (and they prefer to think that he isn't having it with a woman rather than a man), and when she wonders what on earth he sees in you, sex is going to be just about the last thing that she will think of. Unlike her pig of a husband, her boy isn't motivated by that kind of thing. He is the only man in the world who is not.

Flaunting your sexual relationship with her boy is the best way of raising his mother's blood pressure. Luring him into a quickie before you go over to visit her, or making him an explicit promise of good times to be had on your return will guarantee his attentiveness while you are in her home. After you have left, she will tell anyone who will listen that you have ruined his life. What she really means is that you have enticed him into bed.

TAKING OVER

Many women are tempted to complain that as soon as we have a steady relationship with a man, all his responsibilities are ceded to us. They are the small duties that he feels are mere woman's work, and that he is glad to get off his back. But complain no more, because it is in these duties that our power lies. They are not burdens; they are weapons. When his mother decides to interest herself in your monthly mortgage payment, he will not know what it is. Nor will he know how much you have outstanding on credit cards, where your wills are deposited for safekeeping, nor who is the beneficiary of your insurance policy (he had hoped that it might be him, but he's never actually seen the document).

So why is he willing to let you get away with this? Because, by and large, and discounting the occasional despot, if there's one thing that most men hate in this whole world, it's unpleasantness. They would rather sell their soul to the devil than face up to unpleasantness. *They* won't take their suit back to the dry-cleaner when they discover that the creases in the pants run at a 45-degree angle. Nor will they demand satisfaction from the bank teller who accidentally bounced the check for the telephone bill. *We* handle the unpleasantness; control is the reward.

THE FINAL FRONTIER

Is there a better way of handling the problem of men's mothers, you might ask? Well, yes . . . and no. You could try settling down with an orphan; if you can find one, that is. These days most women seem to make a real effort to live long enough to see their sons married to the wrong women. The sad truth is, there's no nice way out. The bottom line of this two-thousand-year-old relationship problem is simply that he has to be trained to fear you more than he fears her. You are more useful to him. There's the sex thing, for starters; and you're the only person who knows where the new rolls of toilet paper are kept.

Of course, where the system breaks down is, now that you've learned how to cope with your mother-in-law, your future daughter-in-law is going to have no chance. She's going to wake up one day to find herself married to a real son-of-a-bitch.

HOW
TO DEKE OUT
MEN

Turn a man's petty, competitive behavior to your advantage. To accomplish this, one requires knowledge of only one simple fact: men will accept any challenge, or take on any task, as long as it is presented to them within a competitive framework. Men just have to win; they have to have the last word. Put it to the test . . . .

You are stopped at an intersection for a red light in the left hand lane, a male driver is stopped in the right hand lane. Wait until there is no traffic or pedestrians in the intersection but make sure the traffic light is still red. Accelerate about three feet forward. The male driver, nine times out of ten, will floor the accelerator and proceed through the intersection on the red light with the smug belief that he beat you to the draw. This is especially rewarding if a traffic policeman has witnessed the infraction and the creep gets a ticket.

Still not convinced men can be so easily baited? Then try this experiment. Hide a tape recorder in your home, have it ready to record the argument you are about to initiate with your husband, boyfriend or father. Make a statement that you know will annoy him. He will respond. Then tell him that you do not wish to argue, and that's the end of it. He will respond. Tell him that it's typical of his behavior that he always has to have the last word. He will deny it adamantly and tell you that it doesn't bother him in the least not to have the last word. Tell him, "fine." Undoubtedly

he will respond, after which you will repeat "fine." And so on, and so on
. . . . Then play the tape recording for him the next time he denies having
to have the last word on every subject.

There are many experiments to try to manipulate stupid male
behaviour that women can do at home in their spare time. For a complete
catalogue of these, call 555-1212.

THE COMMUNICATION GAP

Let's be frank; men and women are *never* going to understand each other. Men complain that this is because women are illogical and can't handle straight talk. Men are big on telling it like it is, while women simply get confused and emotional.

Inevitably, during any difference of opinion, the discussion will break down and become mere bickering; before you know it, it has turned into a full-fledged row. This is where he wanted you all along. Now he can really tell it like it is.

As usual, he is just looking for an excuse to browbeat you — providing him with further proof of his pure logic and rapier intellect and of your emotional incontinence. Once he has accomplished this to his satisfaction, unlike you, he will forget that the argument ever took place. He will be astounded when, half an hour later as he tries to cuddle up to you on the sofa, you send him away with a flea in his ear. You are "holding a grudge" — more proof of emotional instability.

But the fact is that women don't understand men because men do not make themselves clear. They never say what they mean, and they rarely mean what they say.

For instance, when the man in your life declares, "Buddy just called. He was wondering if I wanted to go over to his place to watch the game,"

he really means, "I called Buddy at work this afternoon to see if I could go over to his place and watch the game. How annoyed are you going to be about being left at home alone for the third time this week?"

No matter how you respond, you are in trouble. If you don't complain, he will take advantage of you. He will almost certainly go out again tomorrow. If you admit that you are annoyed, he will claim he doesn't understand why; it's not as if you had plans to do anything together. Well . . . sex, maybe, but you can do that later after he gets back. As long as he sticks to just four or five beers that is.

When he finally does get home — after midnight and a couple of six-packs — he will wake you out of a deep sleep (he knows you have an eight-thirty breakfast meeting with an important client) to tell you that he loves you. This is another ruse.

When a man says "I love you" it's time to wonder what he's done wrong. Although your first thought might be that he's had an affair or lost the money you put in a joint savings account gambling on the lottery, you will usually discover that he simply wants to get himself out of a tight spot. It's just his way of saying "I know I haven't spoken to you all evening, but are you in the mood for sex, anyway? . . . ," or "I've accepted an invitation to dinner at my mother's without checking with you first," or, simply, "I'm too lazy to get out of my chair, so will you get me another beer?"

According to sociologists, men and women argue about three things; sex, children, and money. If you can persuade your mate to consult one of these doctors of social ills to set about finding ways to stop the disagreements, you will be no better off.

If you argue about sex, they will send you to a sex therapist (what do these people know about sex that we ordinary folk have not yet discovered, and why are they keeping it secret?). If you argue about the children, they will send the whole lot of you to family counselling, where you get to have your arguments in public instead of in the privacy of your own home. If you argue about money, they will say that you are really arguing about your feelings and they will refer you to a psychiatrist who will help you sort them out. And the man in your life will accept from these professionals what he won't accept from you. Advice. After all he's paid for it; he may as well get some use out of it.

What's really amazing about all of this, though, is that no amount of counselling will ever help him understand why his double talk should leave you so frustrated. When you angrily explain that all you want is some straightforward communication, he accuses you of being hysterical. "I don't understand what it is you want from me," he declares. And at last he has spoken the truth.

Of course, what he really means to say is, "I don't remember what we were arguing about," because for men it's the confrontation that counts, not the content.

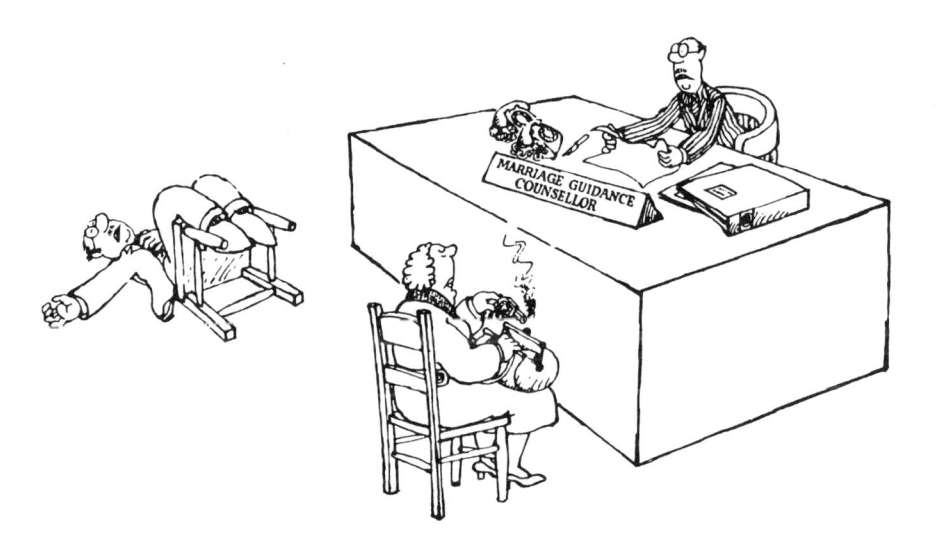

"Well, that's not a very good start is it, Mrs. Murdoch?"

THE SEVEN STAGES OF MAN

Men seem to consider manhood as something that must be built, step by step, beginning in infancy. Here is a list of the seven essentials a male must experience if he is ultimately to be judged a "man."

1. TOILET TRAINING

Boys must become toilet trained and it's not an easy task. Little boys are much harder to train than little girls, but then they are so much more anal retentive. Also, the extra time that they spend taking care of their business is well utilized. It allows them more time to become better acquainted with their penises — which they begin to refer to in the third person.

2. SEXUAL DISCOVERY

The age where little boys discover that they are not just different from little girls, but that they hold a privileged position in the world. They become aware that they will always be paid more, be more politically powerful, and have greater opportunities. They wonder why this is so. The only difference they *see* between themselves and little girls is right there between their legs. They rejoice.

3. LITTLE LEAGUE
(or PeeWee Hockey or any other team sport that excludes girls)

A boy's first truly competitive arena in which to begin building his manhood; here he can prove his masculinity. He learns that winning is everything. Winning the game builds character; ruthless, competitive, male character.

4. PUBERTY

Nothing will ever equal a boy's first orgasm which is usually provided by his five-fingered friend, Mr. Hand. And with his first ejaculation the male stupidity gene is released throughout his body, and unleashed upon the world. Masturbation will have to comfort him until phase five is realized.

5. LOSS OF VIRGINITY

His first sexual experience with someone other than himself. Although there might be some question as to whether or not he had actually been "inside" his partner before achieving the "orgasm that shook the world." Most men are extremely grateful for the opportunity their partner provided them and they will always remember her fondly. The woman, however, thinks that this extremely brief episode is probably best forgotten.

6. ARRESTED ADOLESCENCE AND SEXUAL PEAK

Achieved in unison around the age of 18. During this phase a young man learns that there is more to life than penetration, thrust, and ejaculation; there is ruthless male competition at an Ivy League school, there are Visa, Mastercard, and American Express. There are Corvettes and Trans-Ams, Club Med, and "Monday Night Football." He also learns that honesty is something he likes in his women, but not in himself. Anything a man tells a woman during this phase of his life should be taken with a grain of salt — and a quart of tequila.

7. FATHERHOOD

The phase where he pursues a career, then meets, falls in love, and marries a woman, buys an RRSP, procreates, gets deeply in debt, and finally dies — but not before he teaches his son all that he knows about the seven stages of manhood.

A man experiencing the seventh and final phase of "Manhood"

EVERY MAN'S IDEAL WOMAN

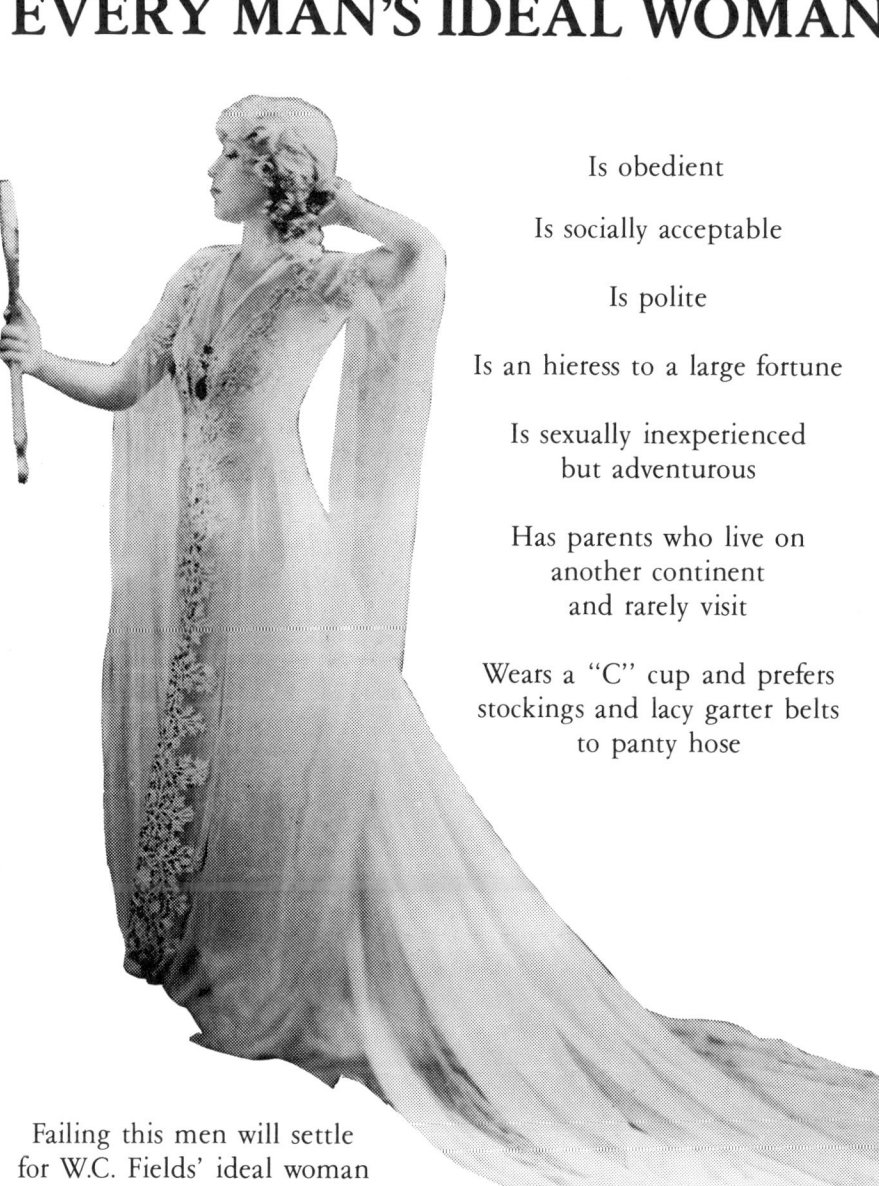

Is obedient

Is socially acceptable

Is polite

Is an hieress to a large fortune

Is sexually inexperienced
but adventurous

Has parents who live on
another continent
and rarely visit

Wears a "C" cup and prefers
stockings and lacy garter belts
to panty hose

Failing this men will settle
for W.C. Fields' ideal woman
"dumb, over-sexed,
and owns a liquor store"